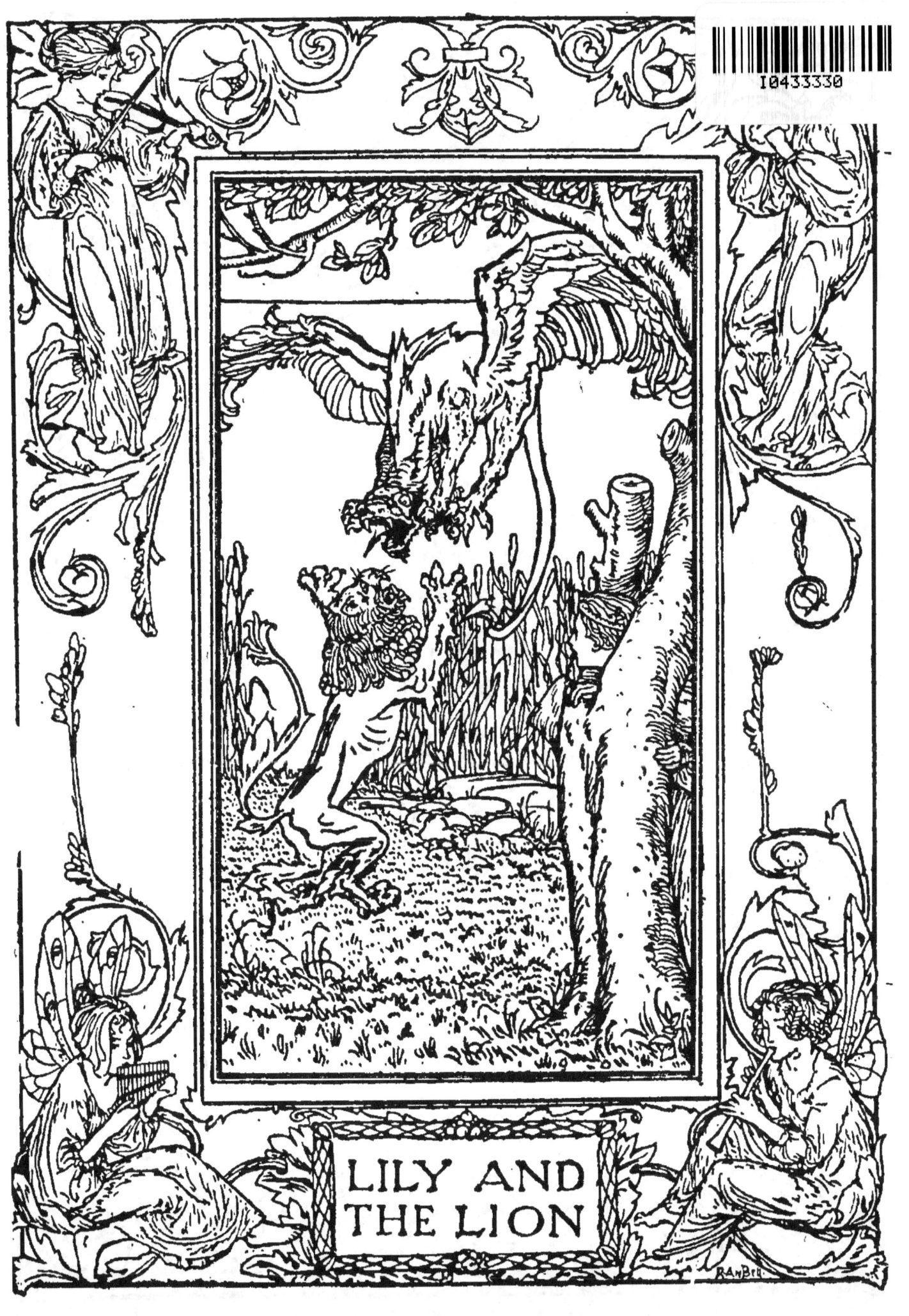

LILY AND THE LION

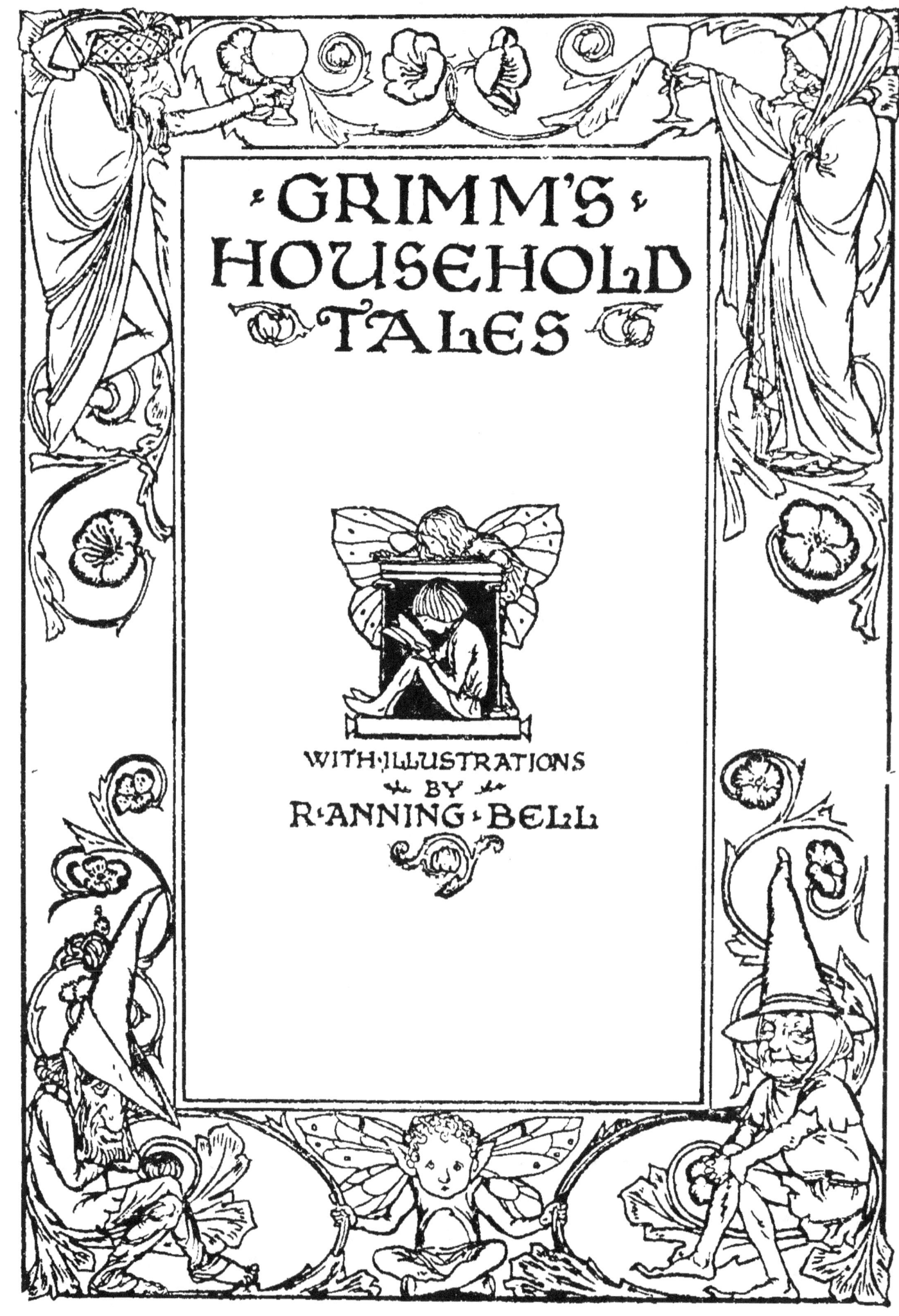

GRIMM'S HOUSEHOLD TALES

WITH ILLUSTRATIONS
BY
R. ANNING BELL

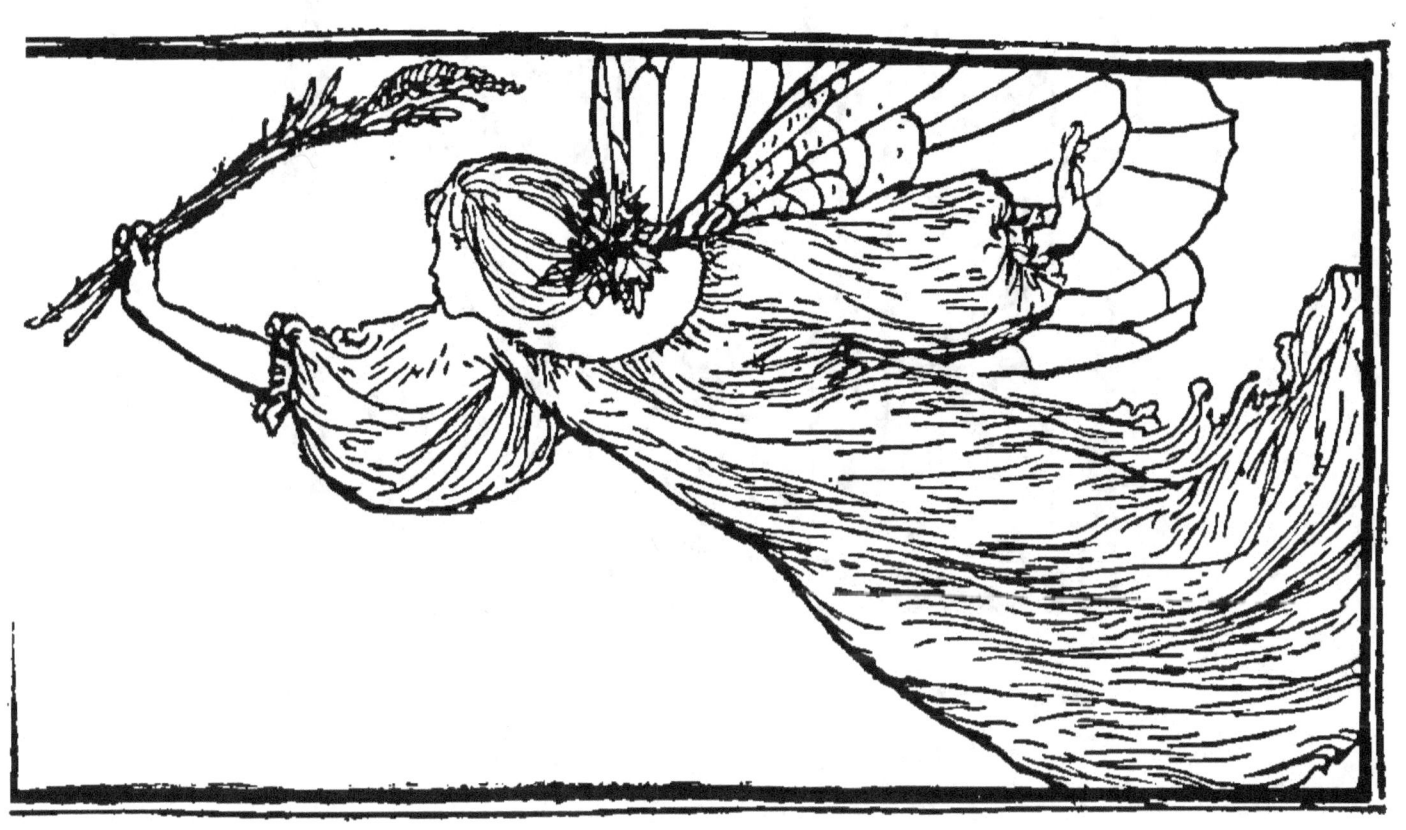

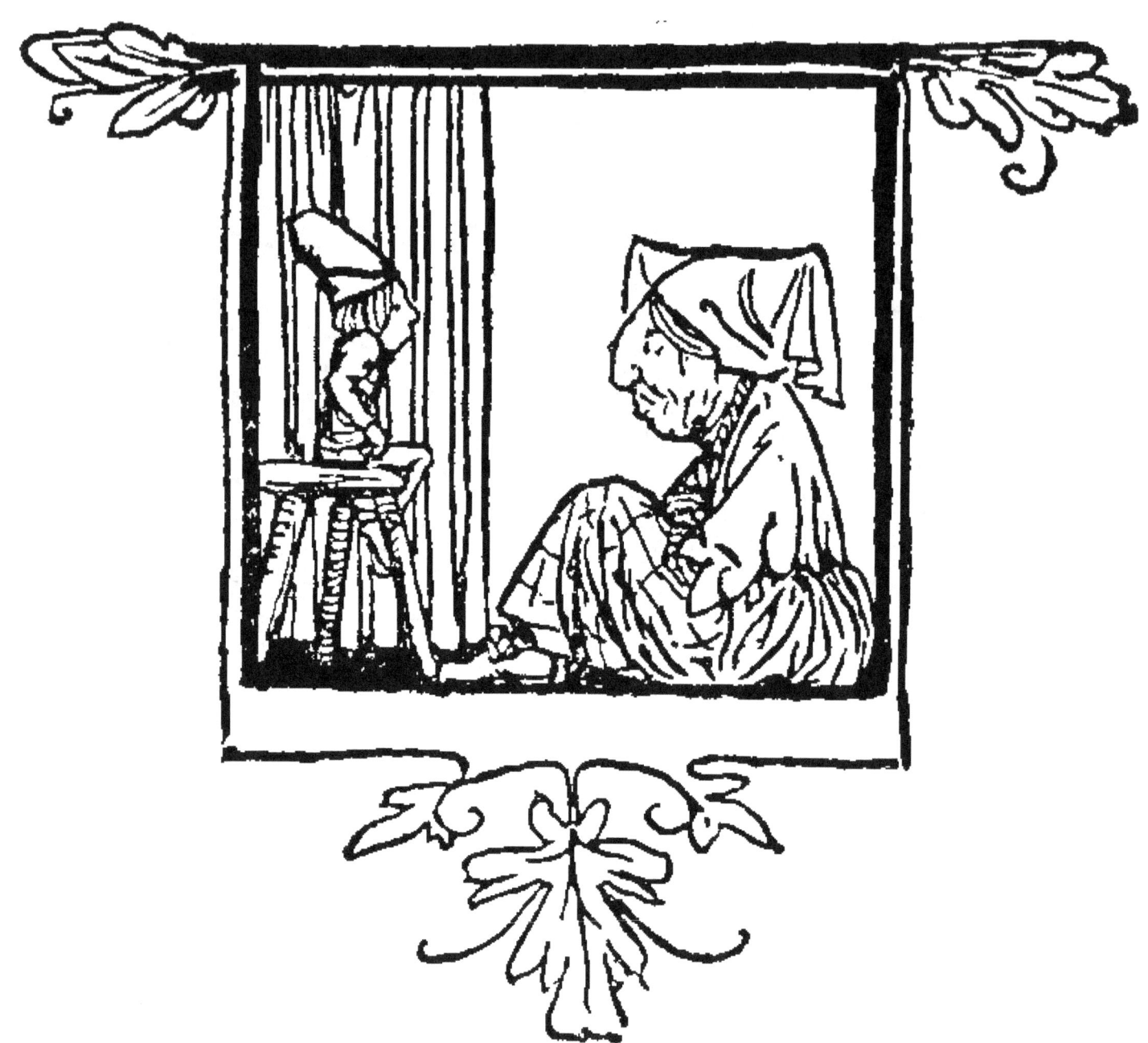

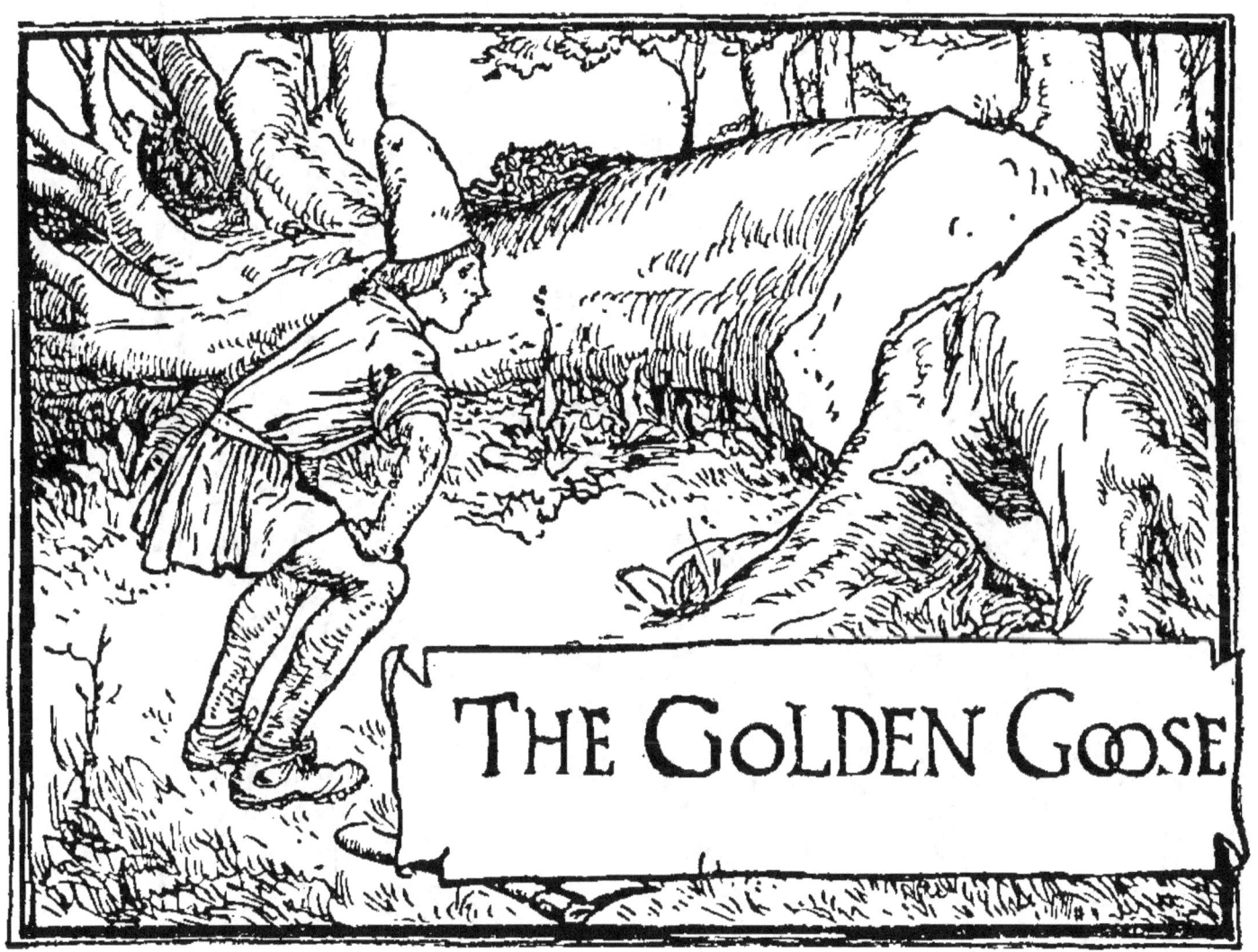

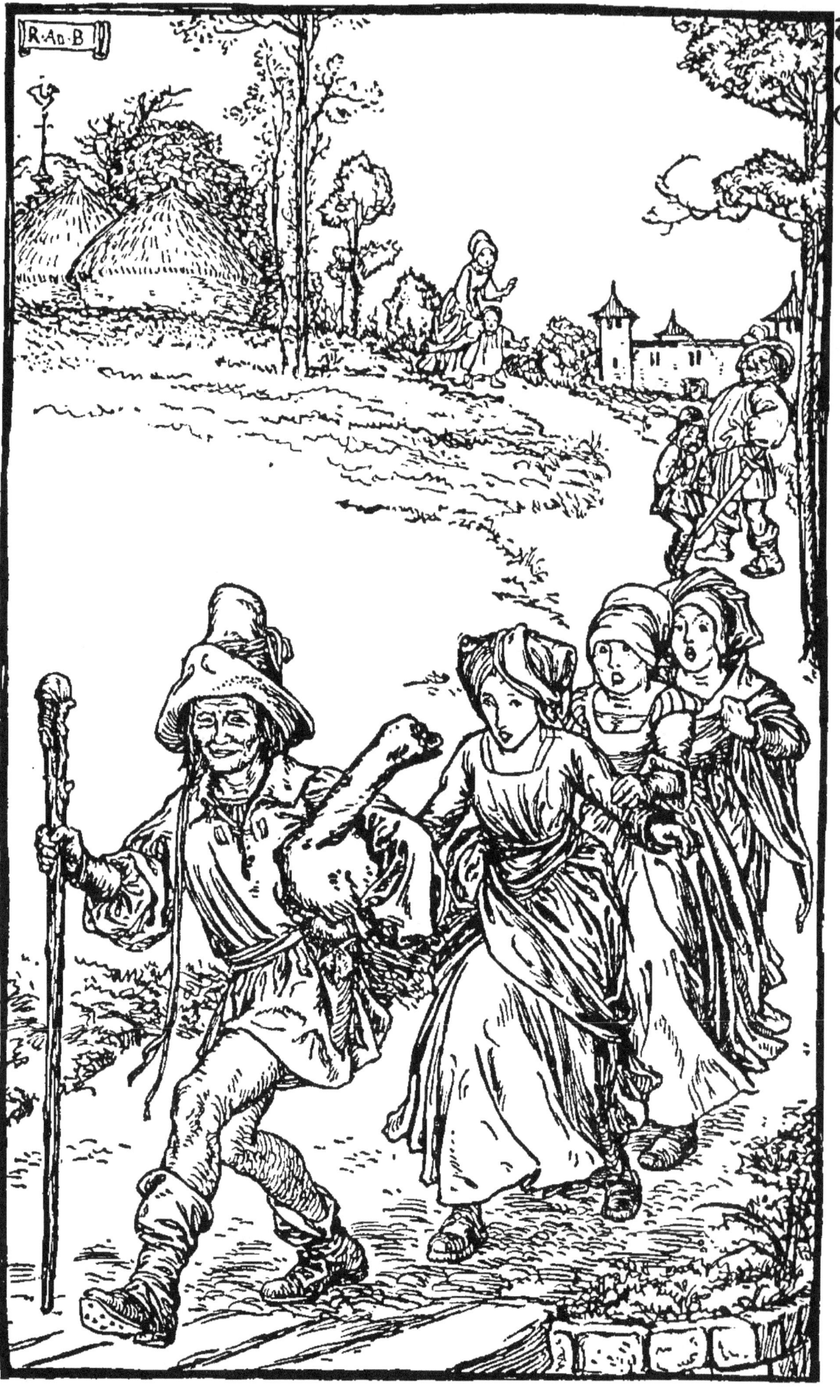

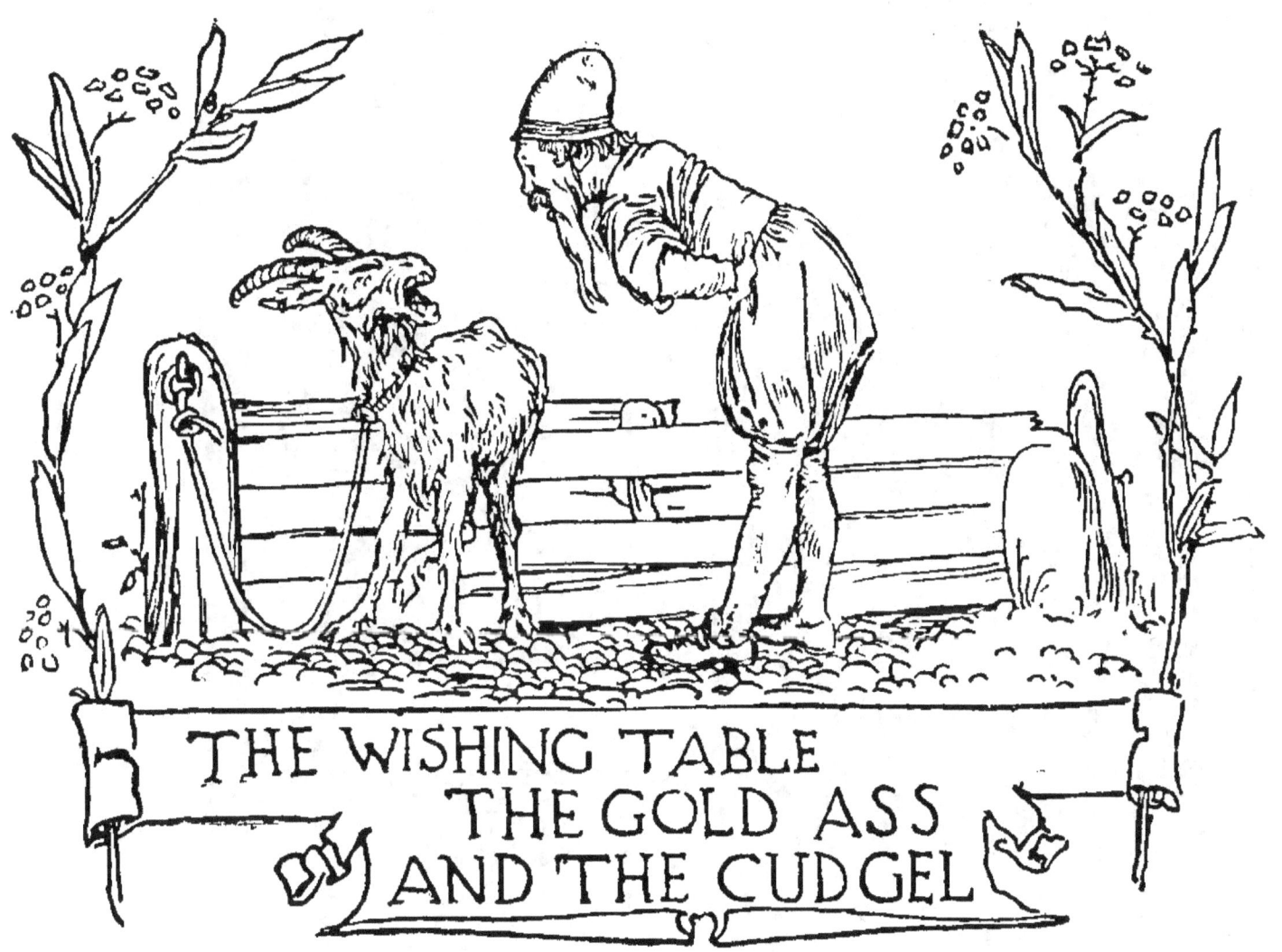

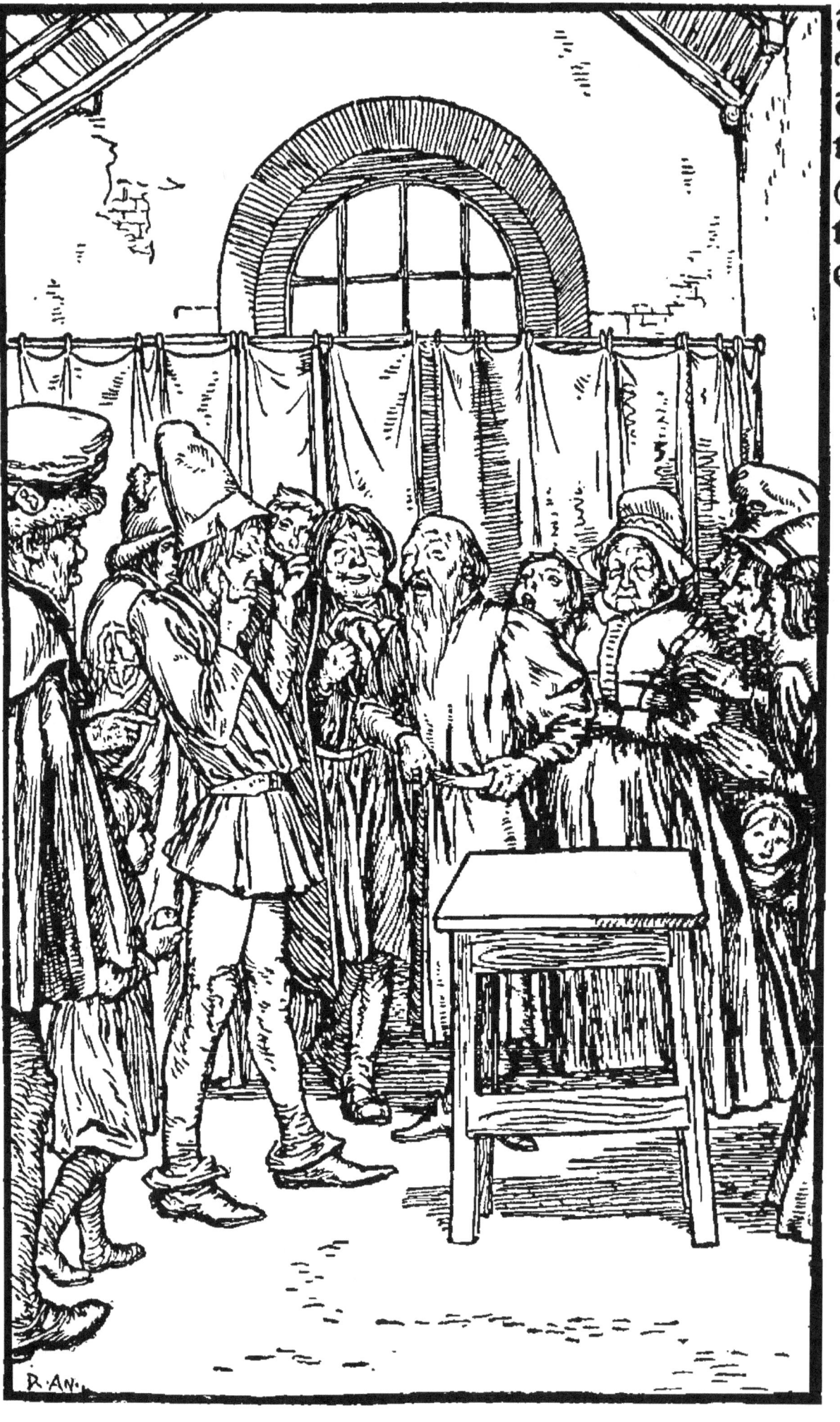

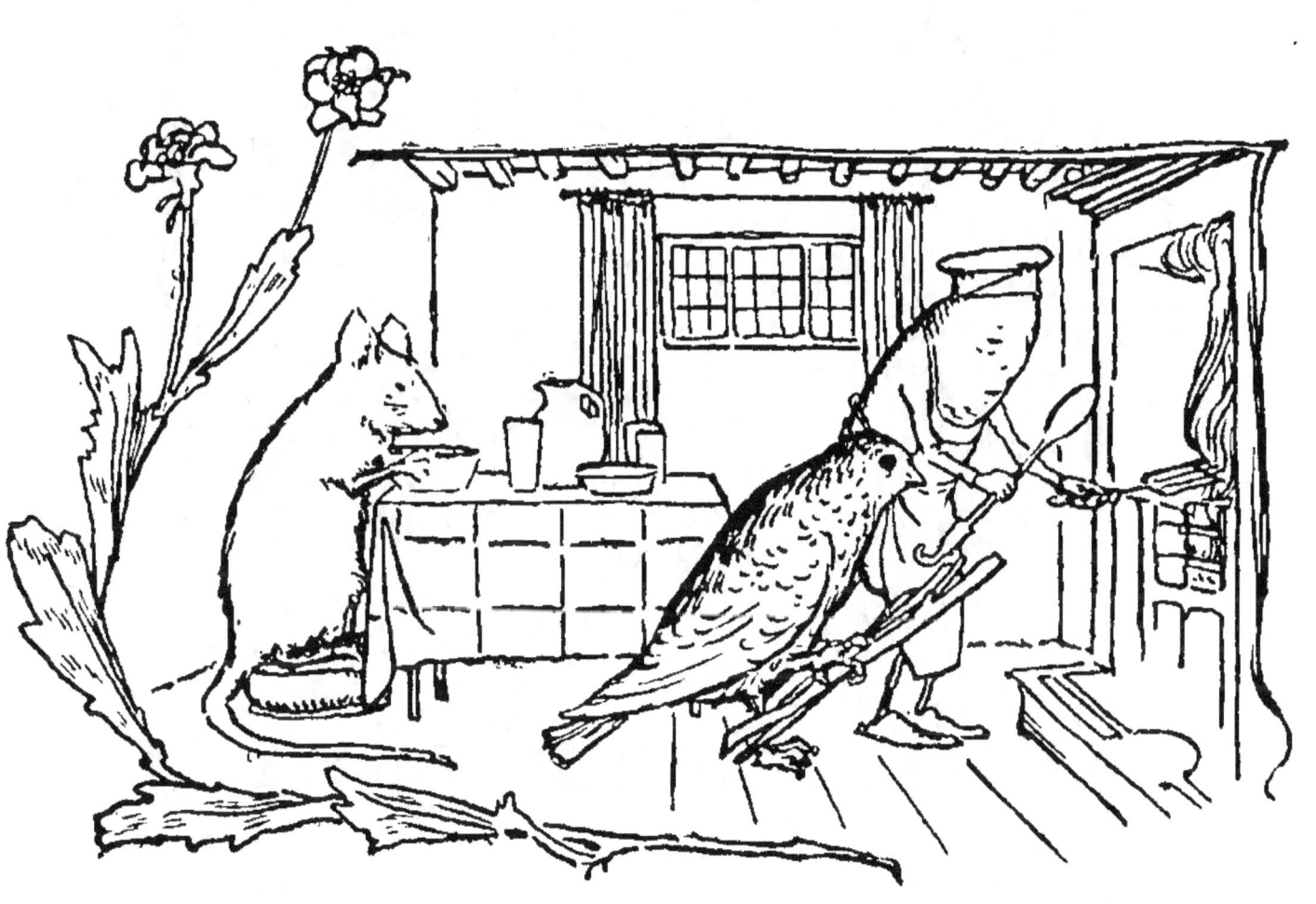

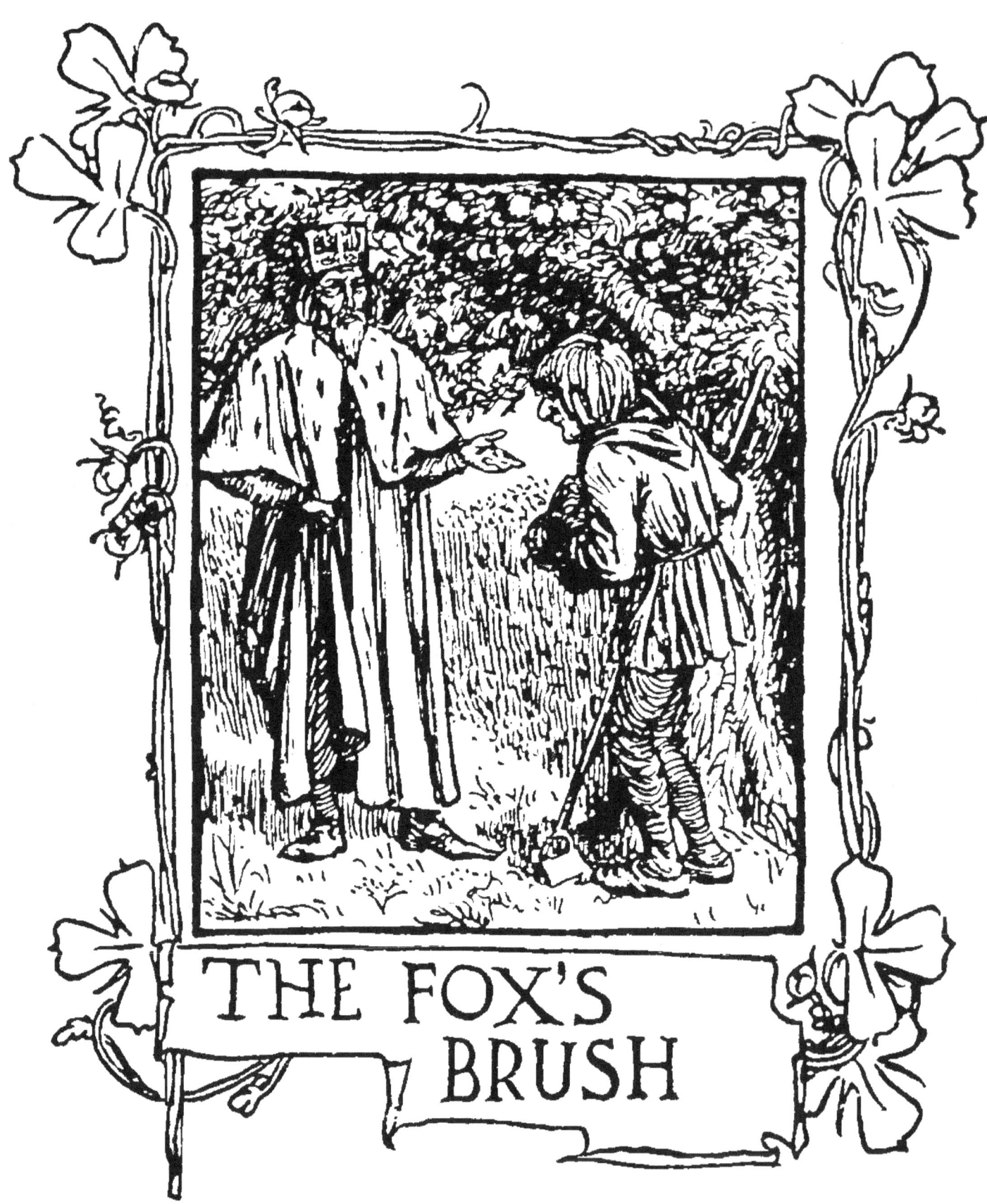

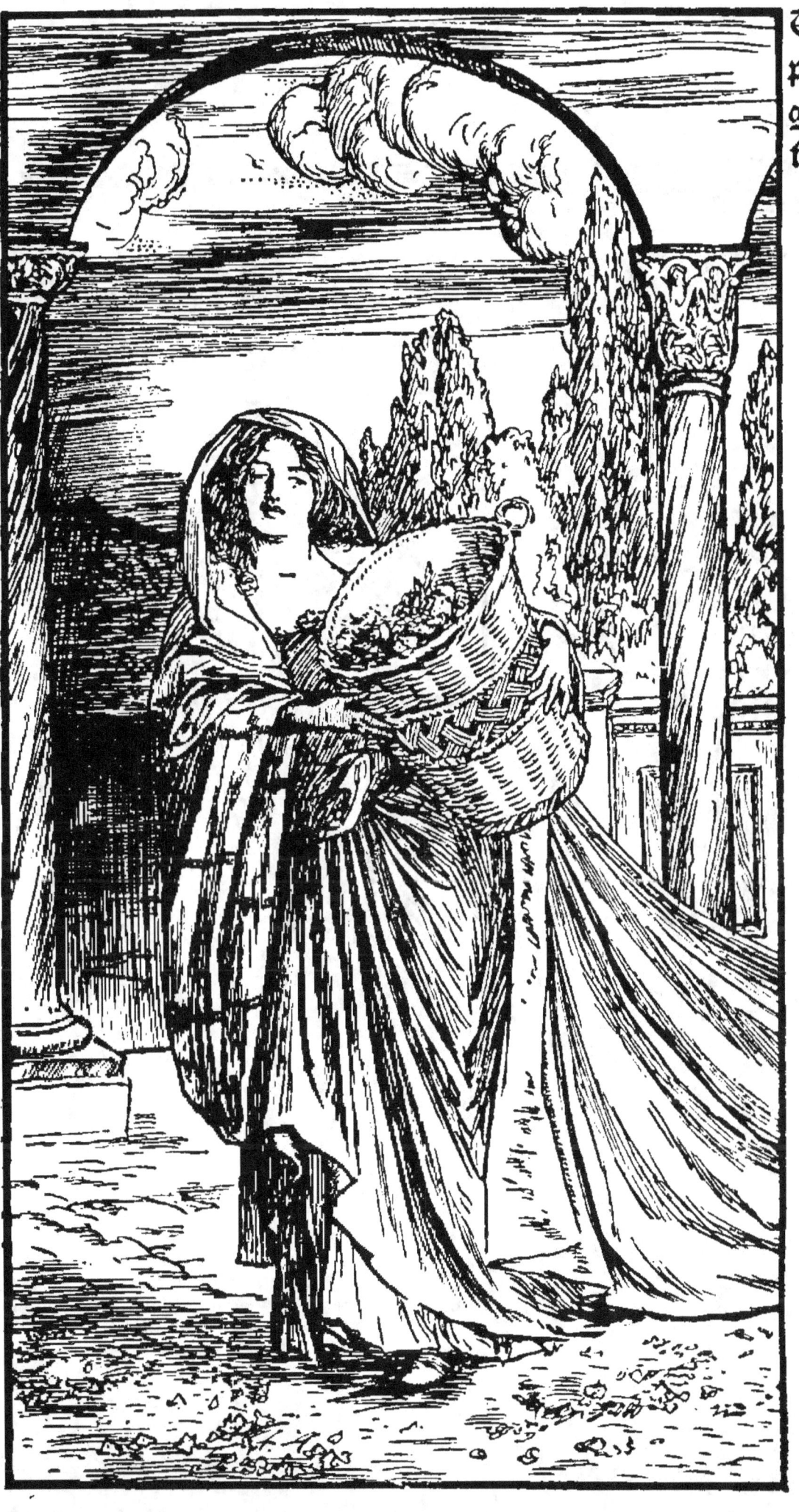

The princess going to the bath

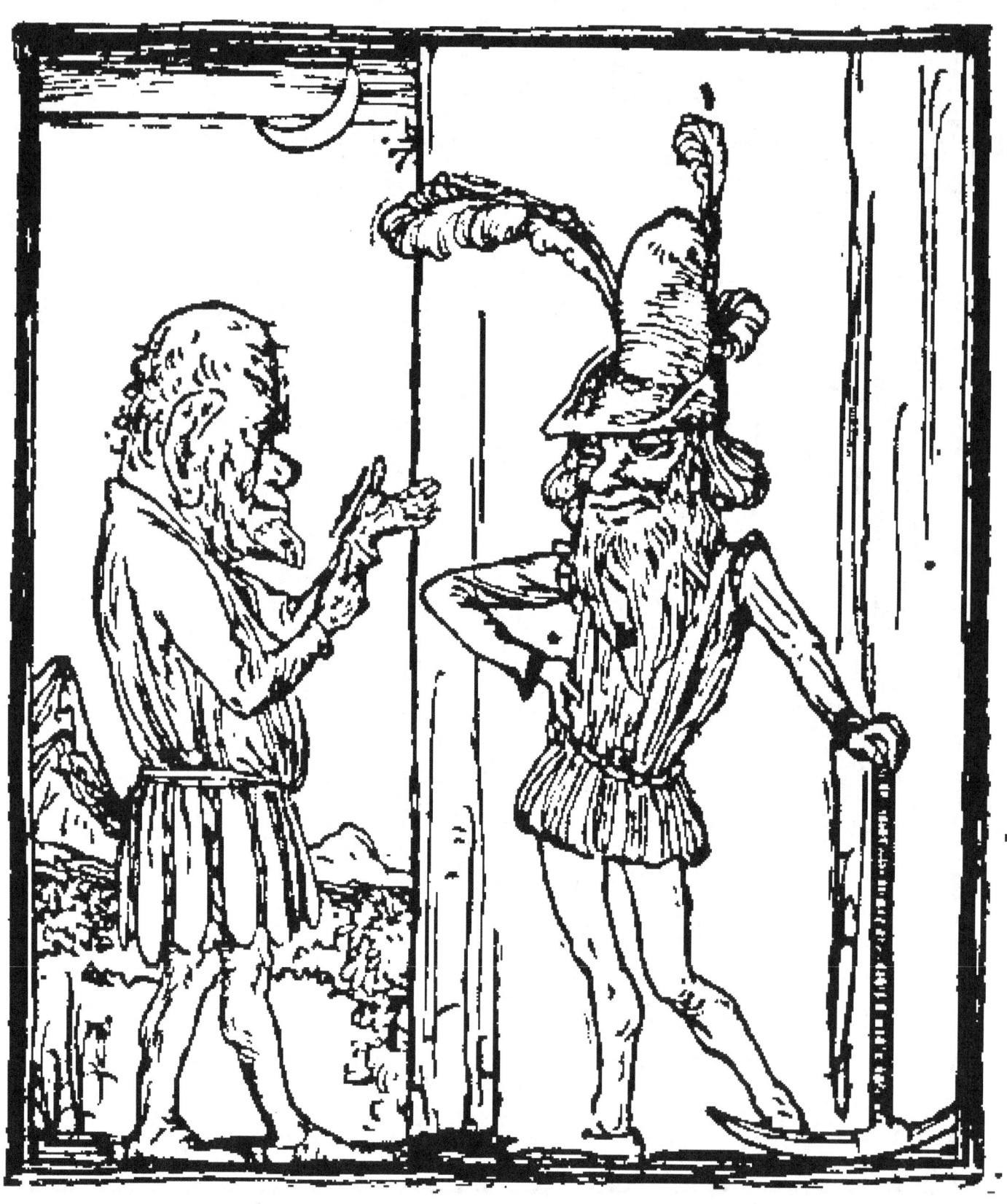

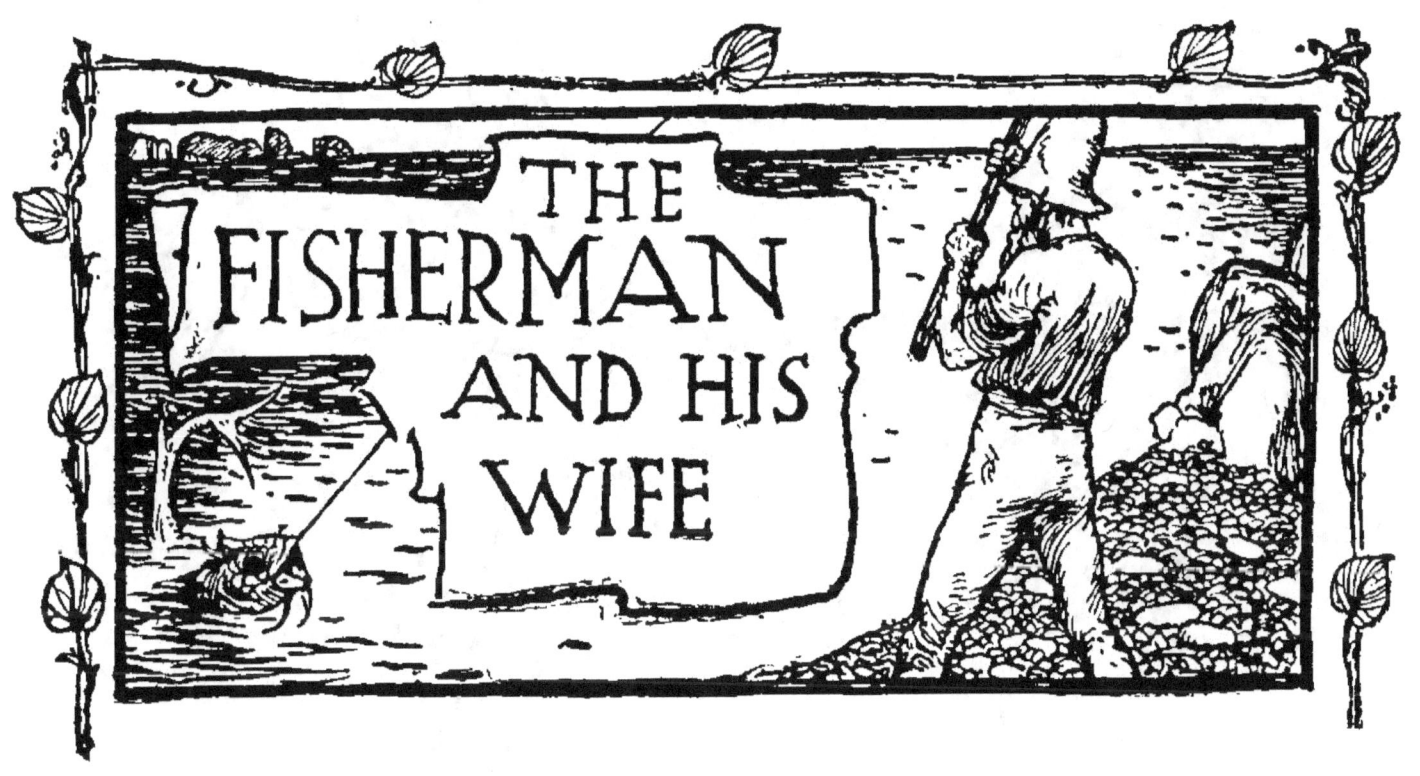

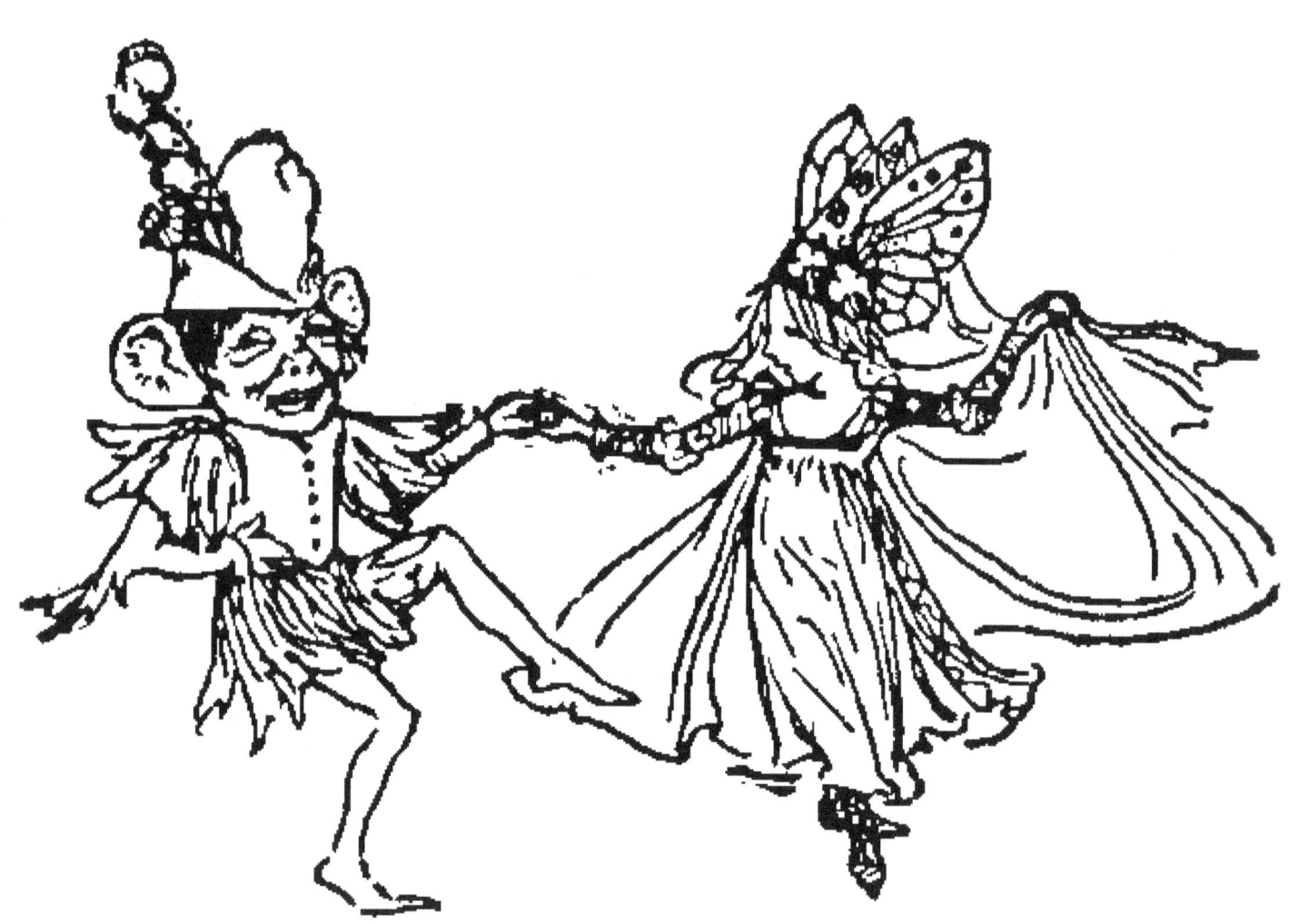

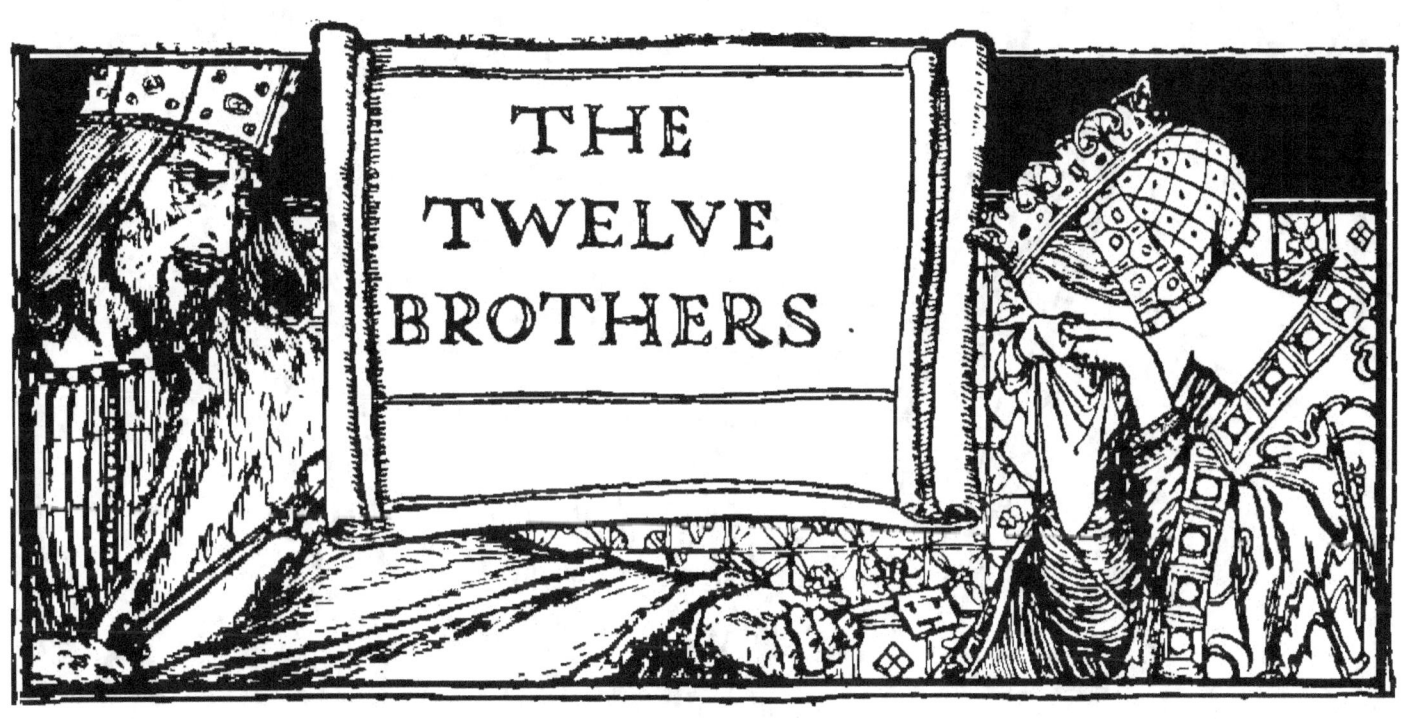

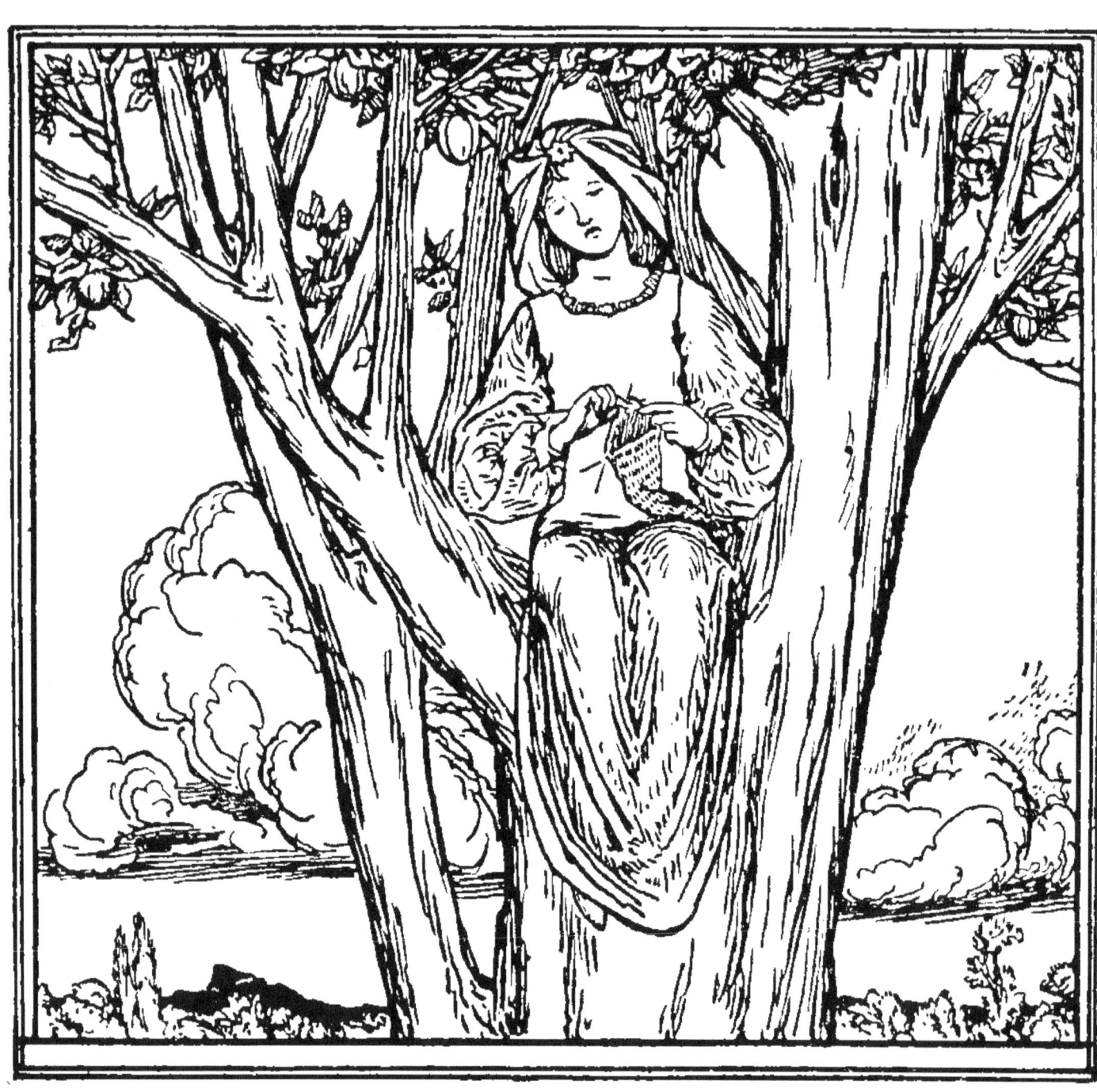

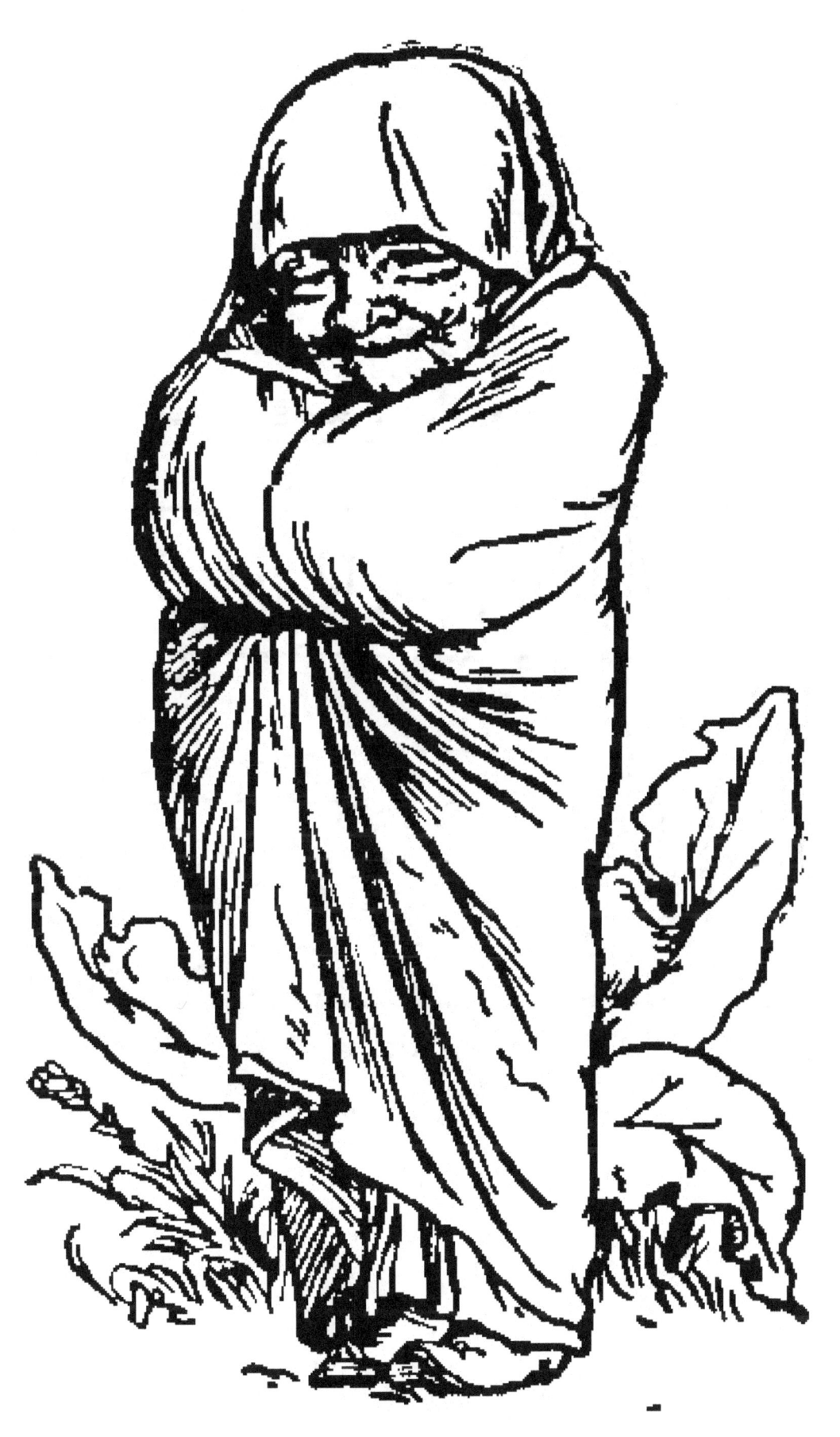

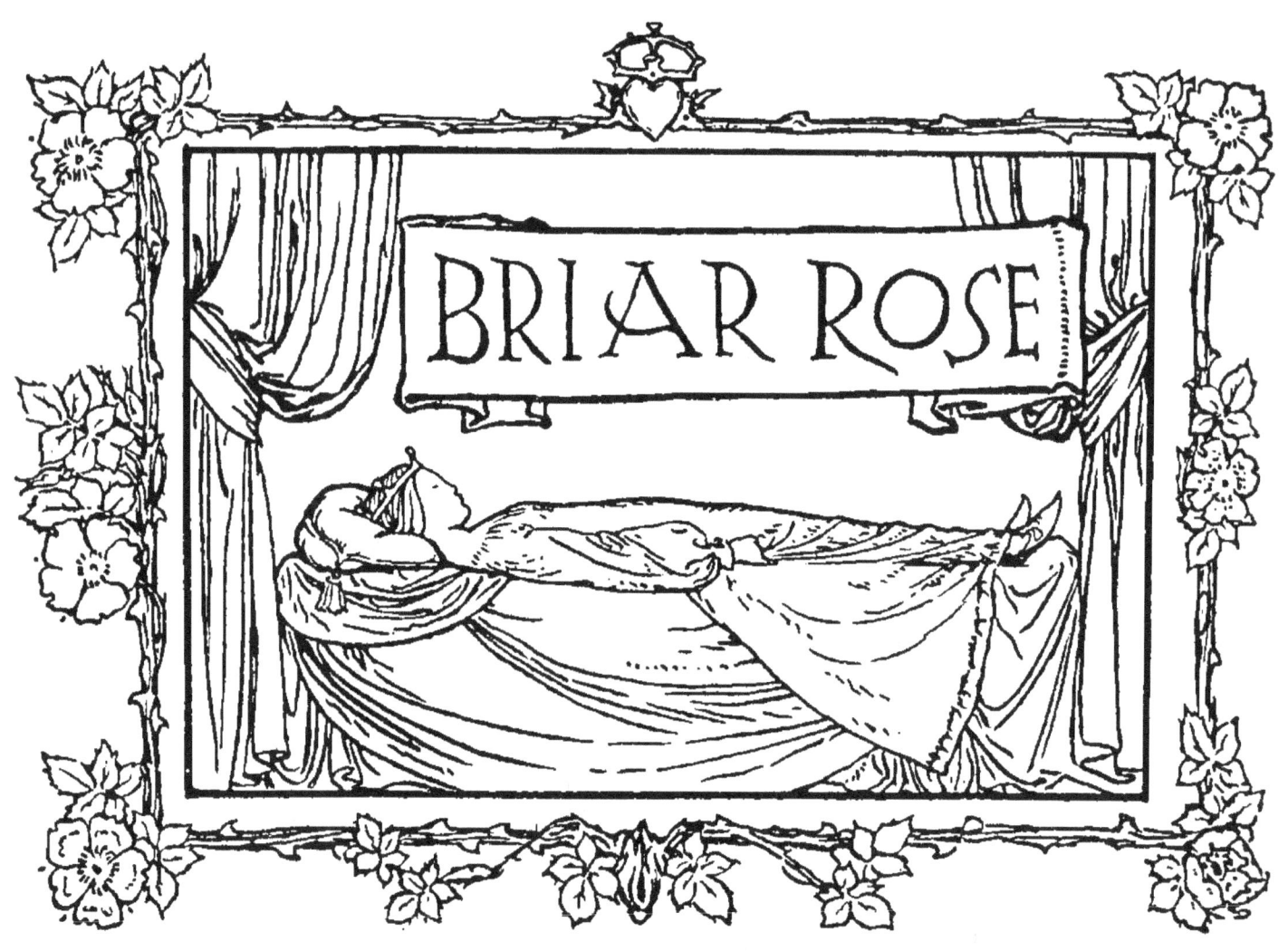

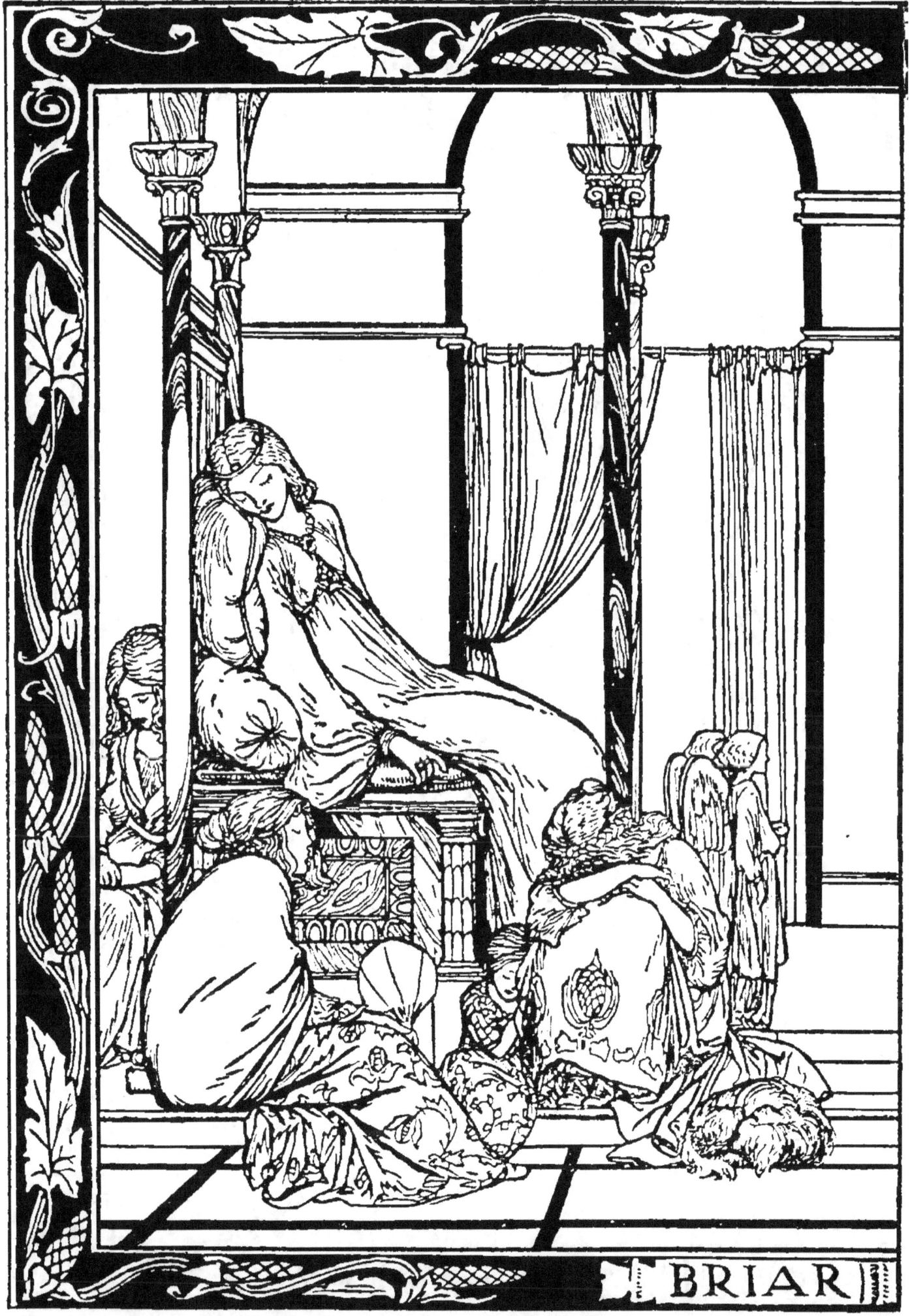

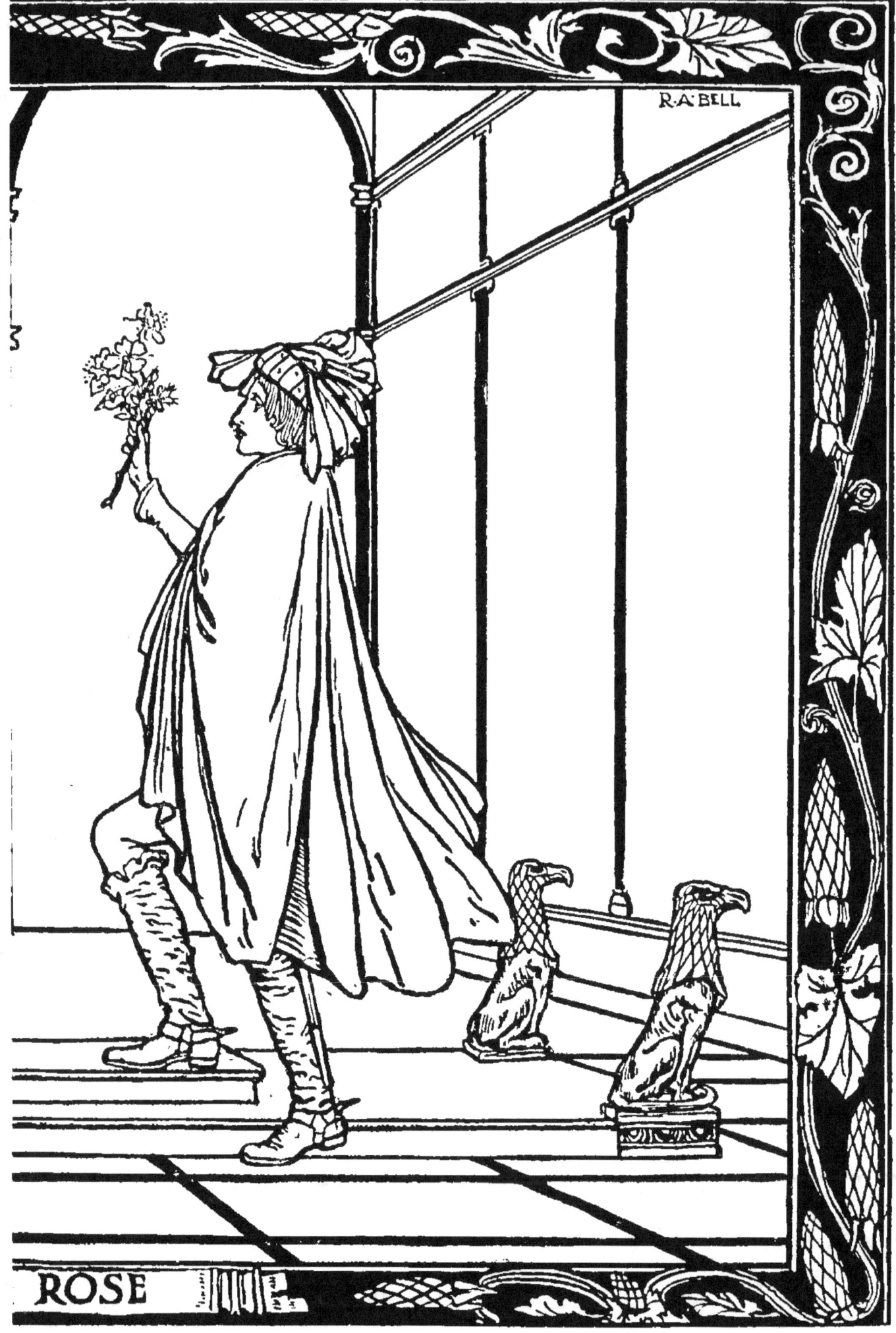

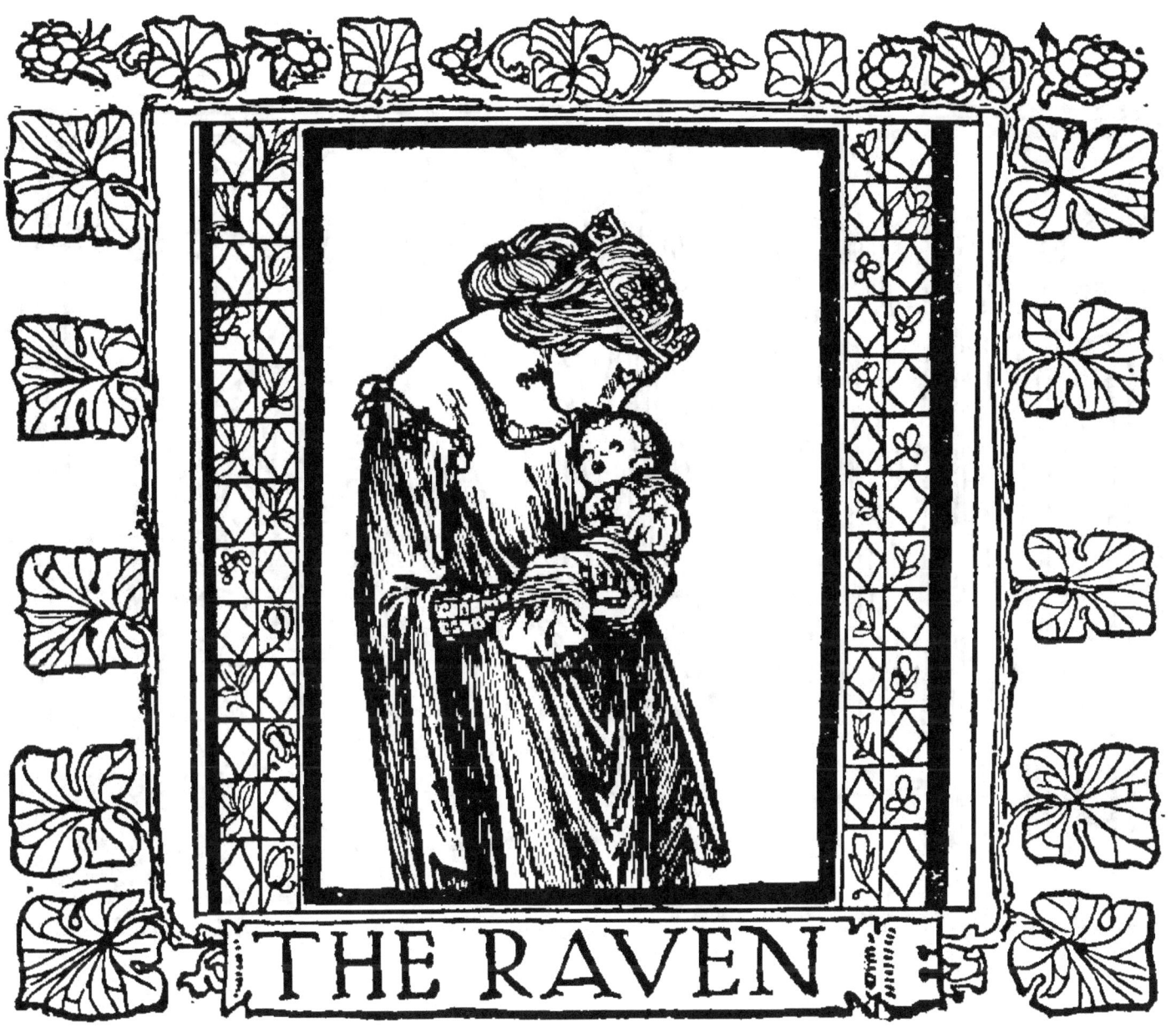

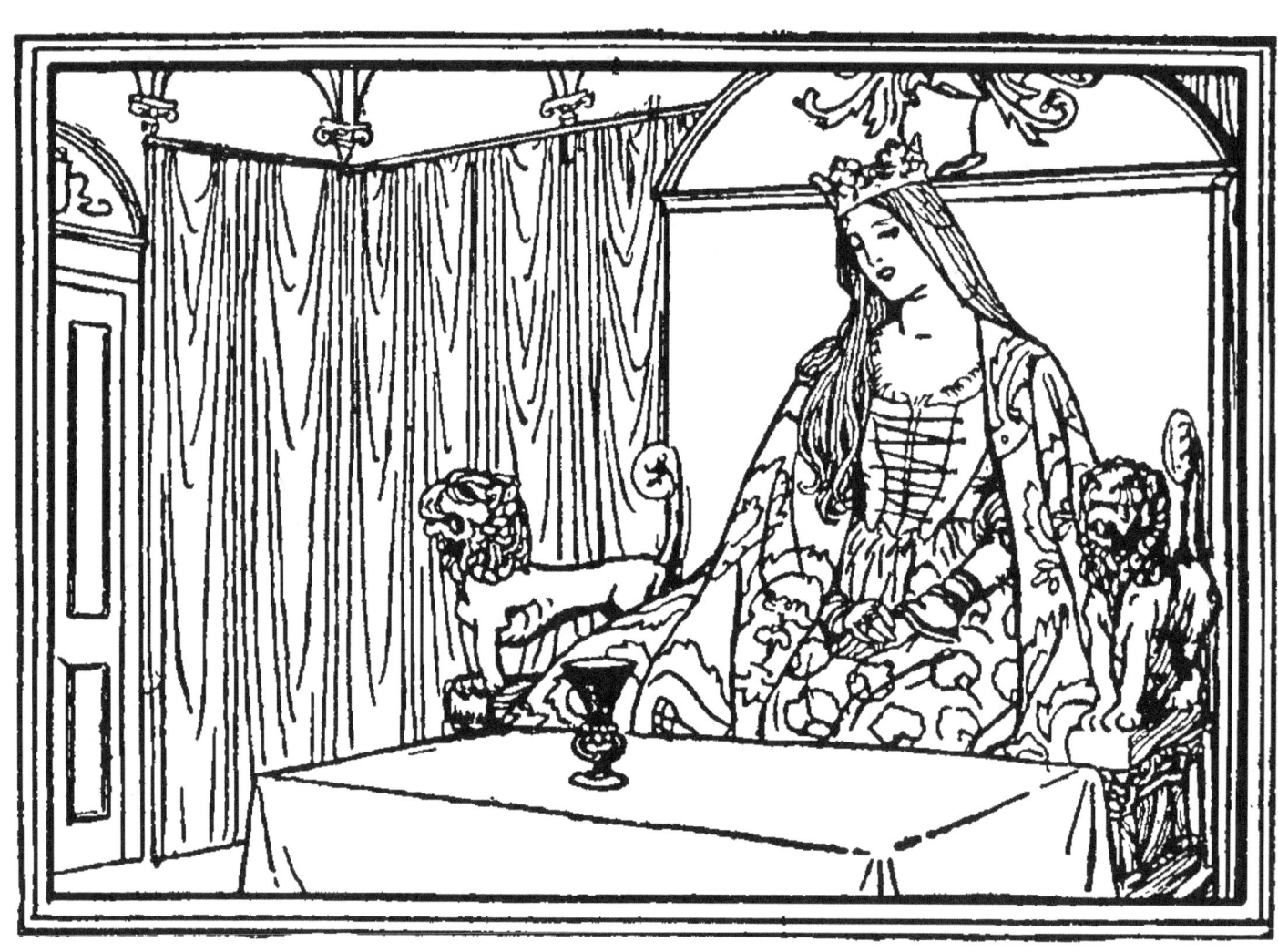

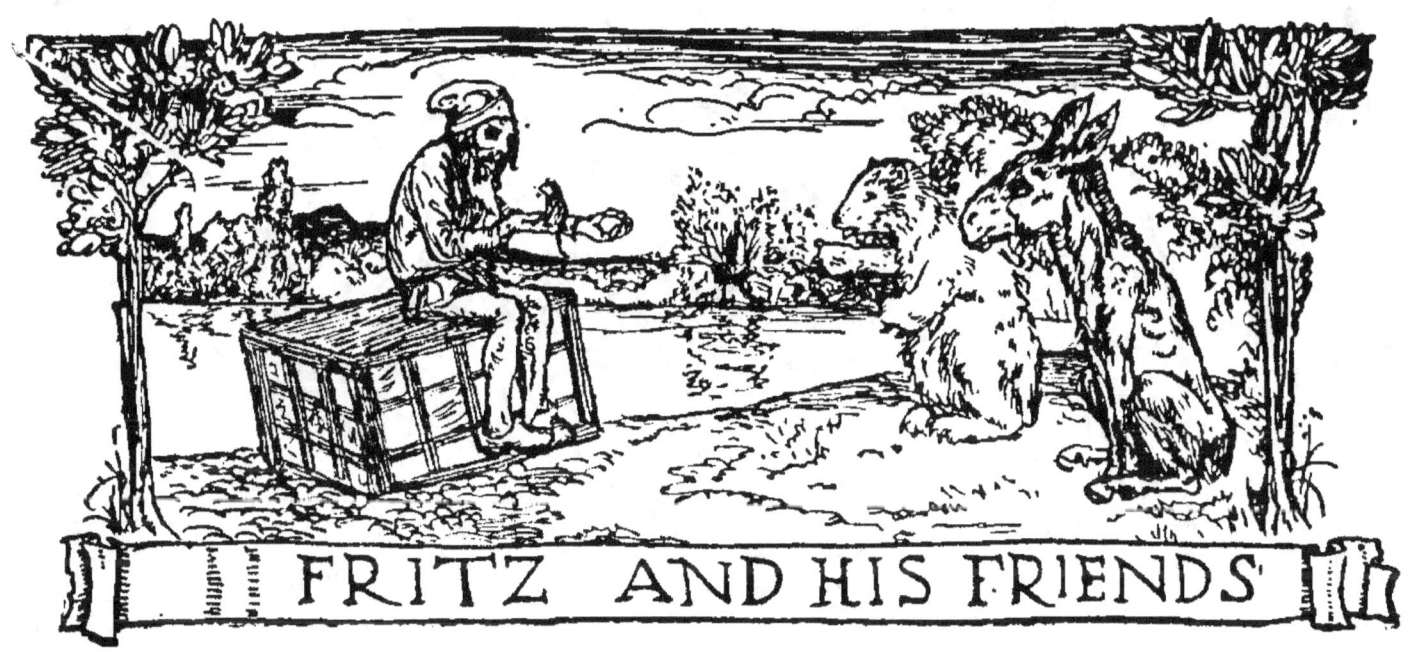

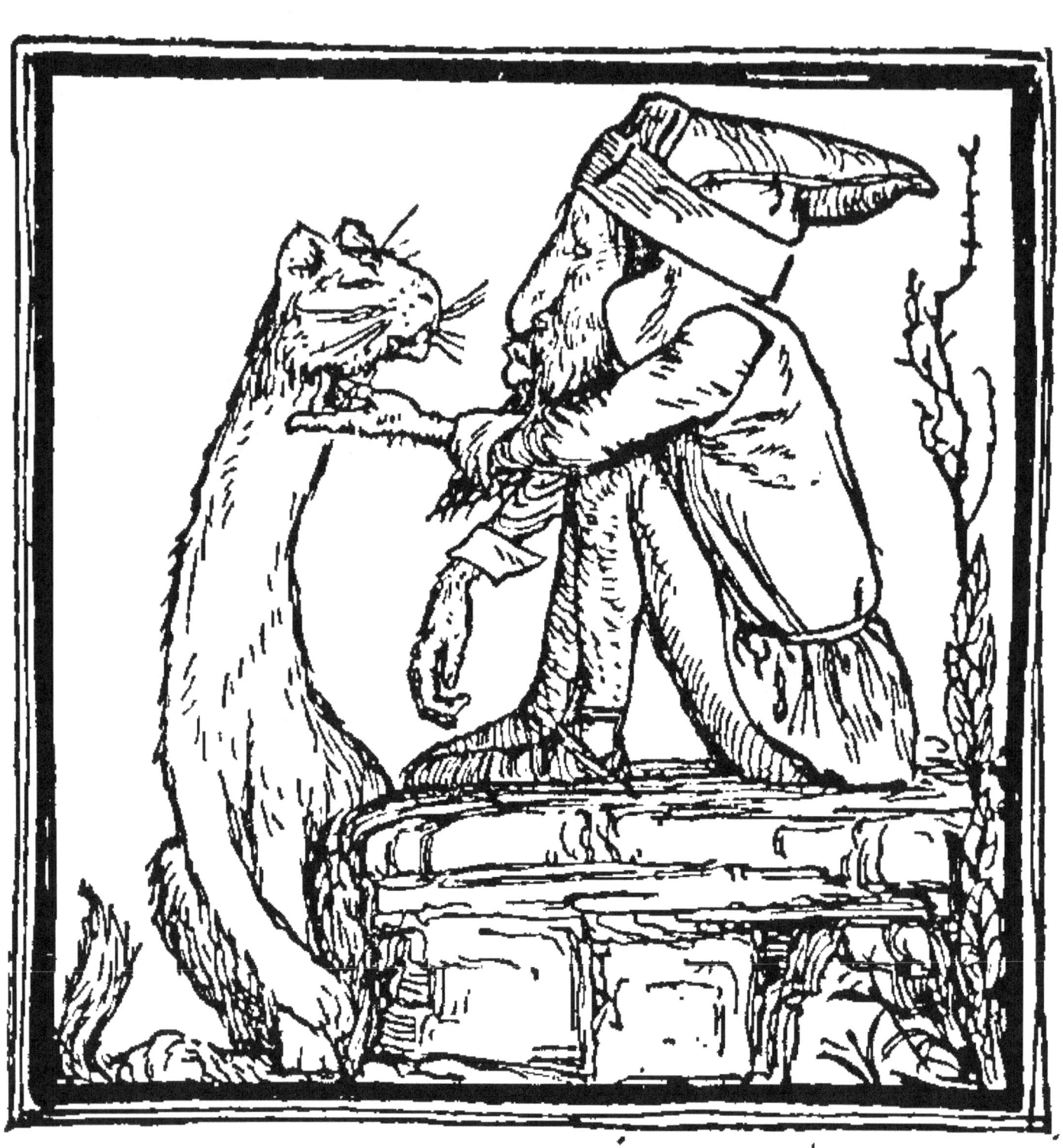

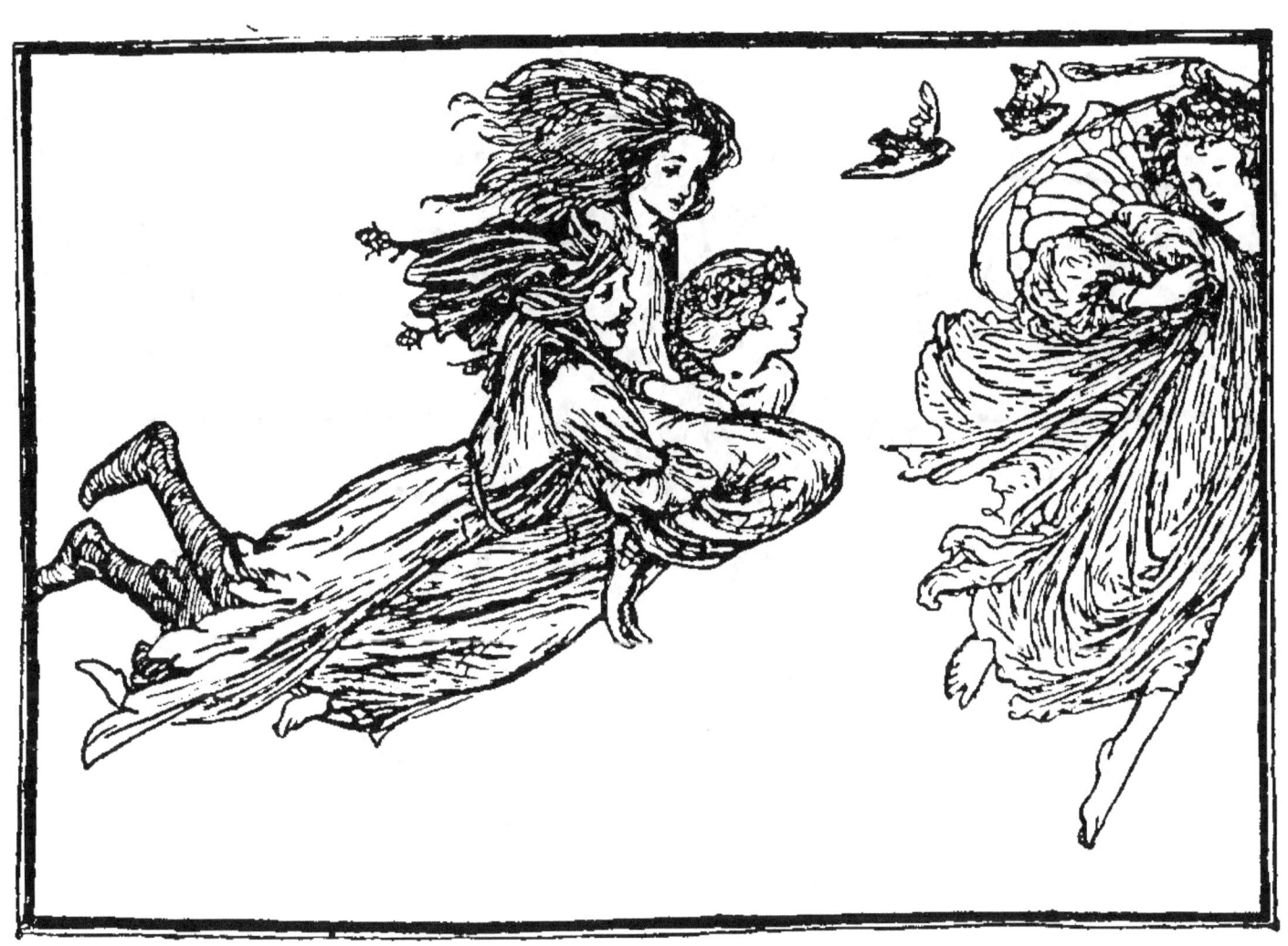

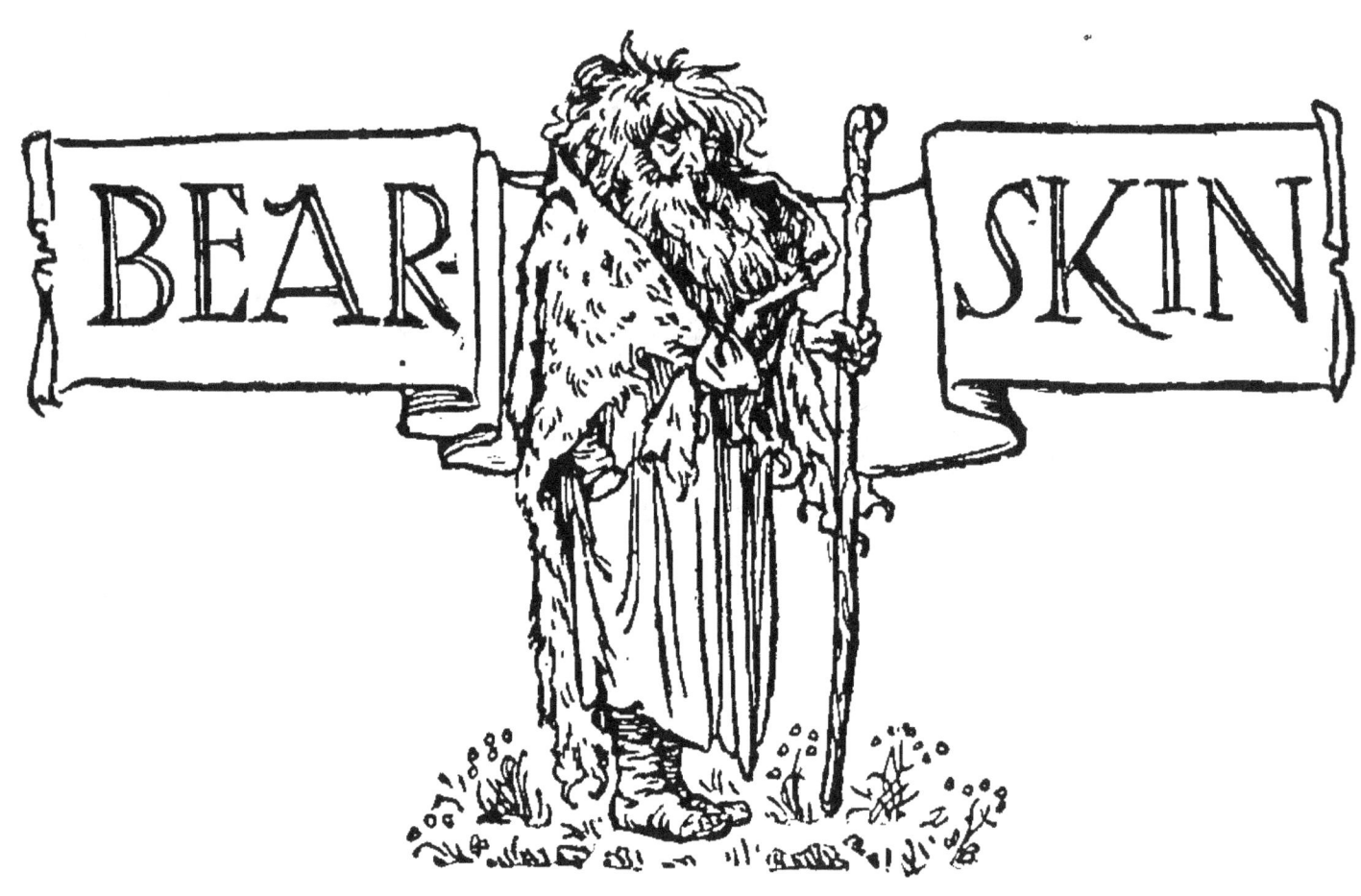

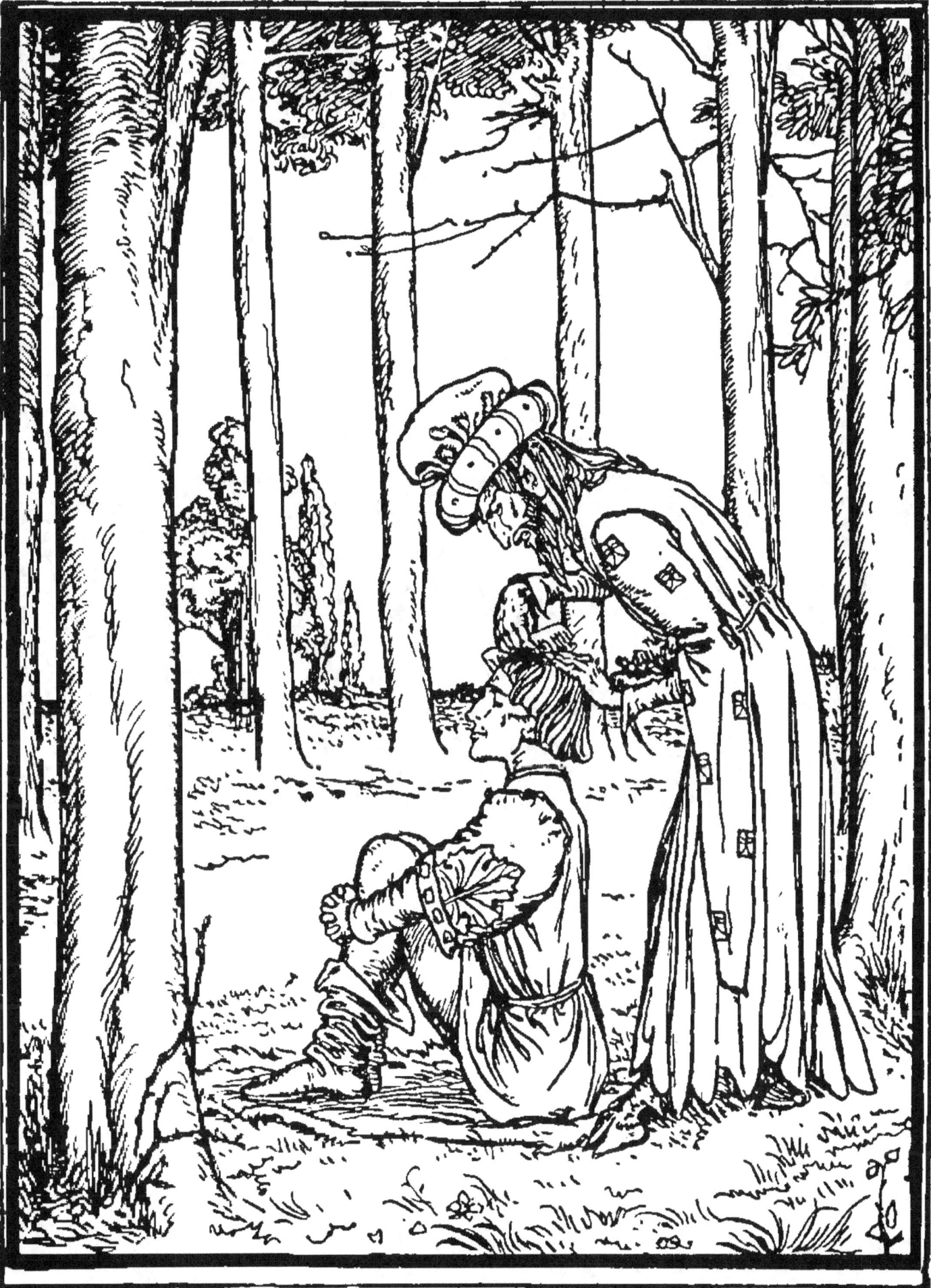

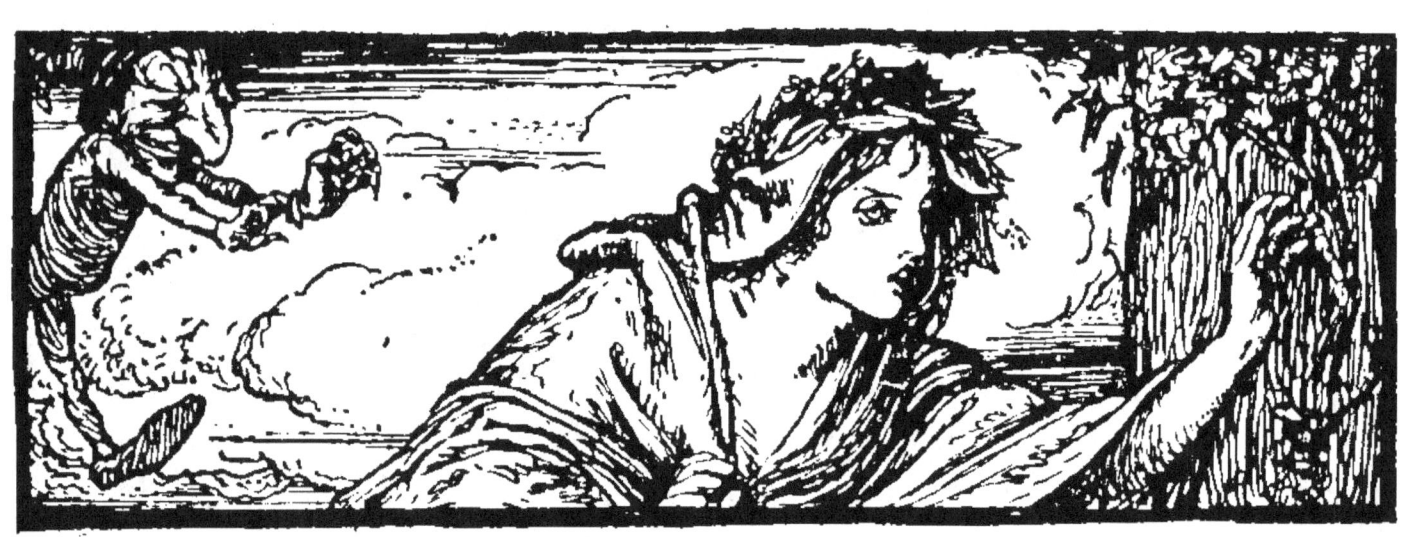

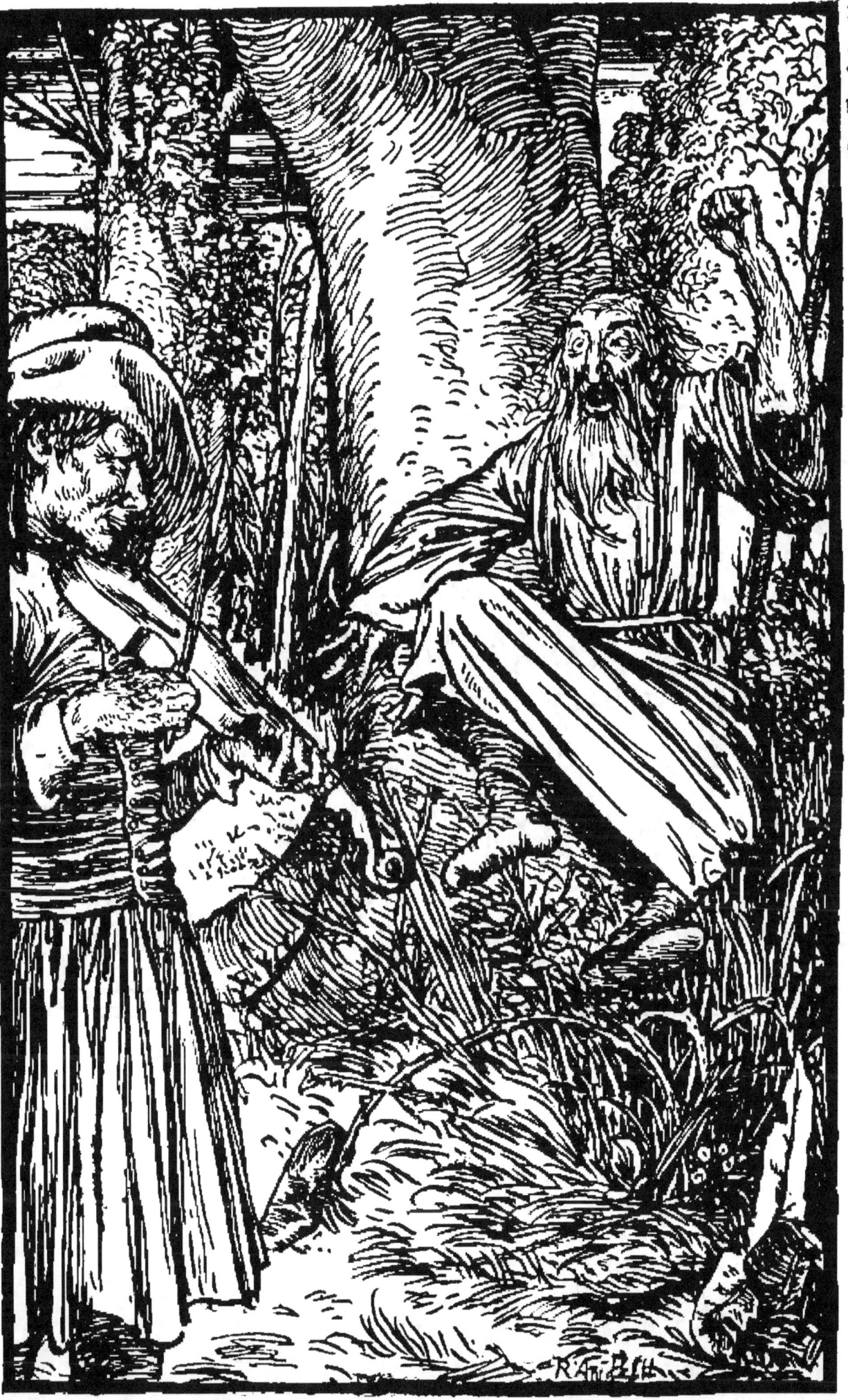

The Jew in the Bush

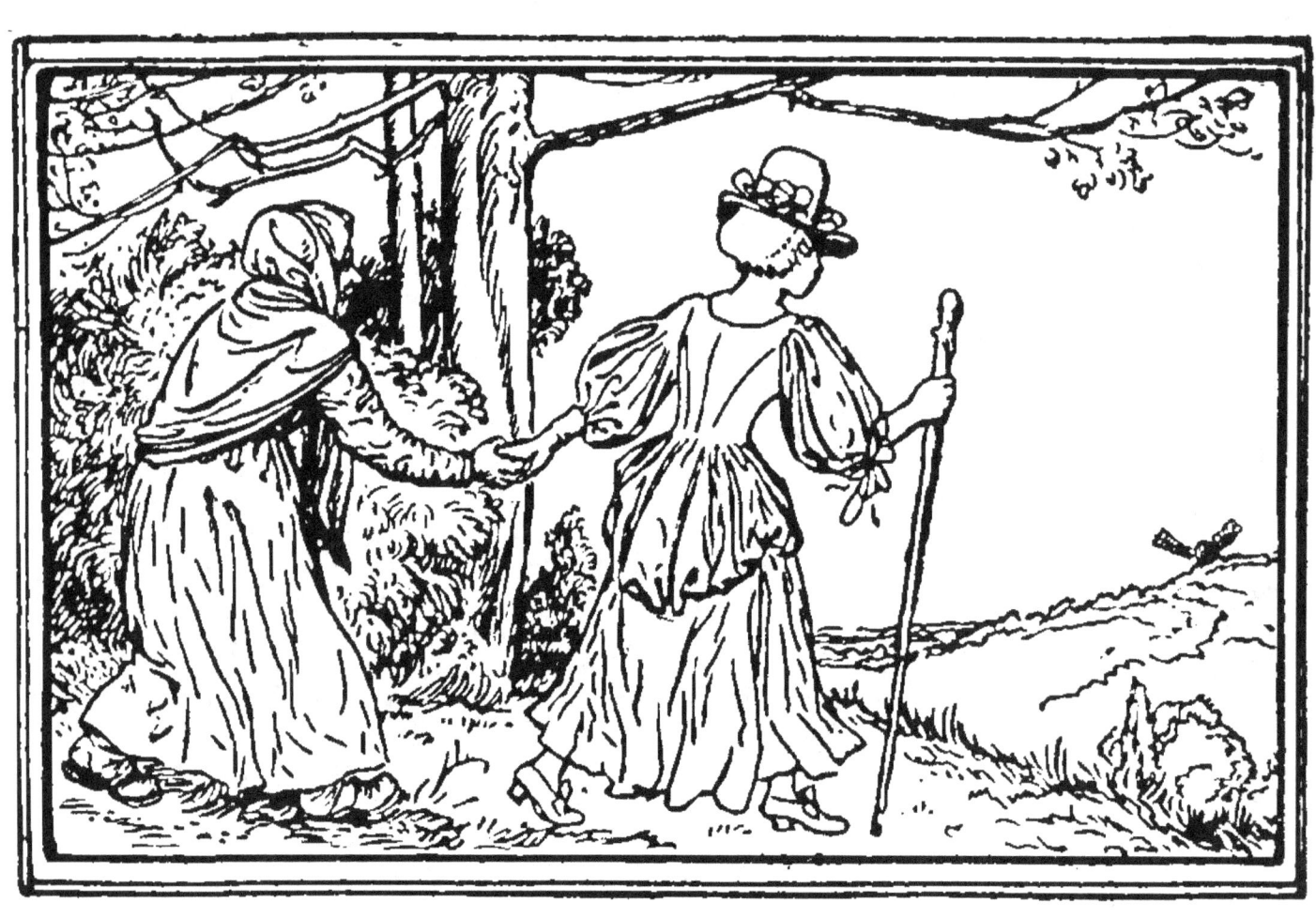

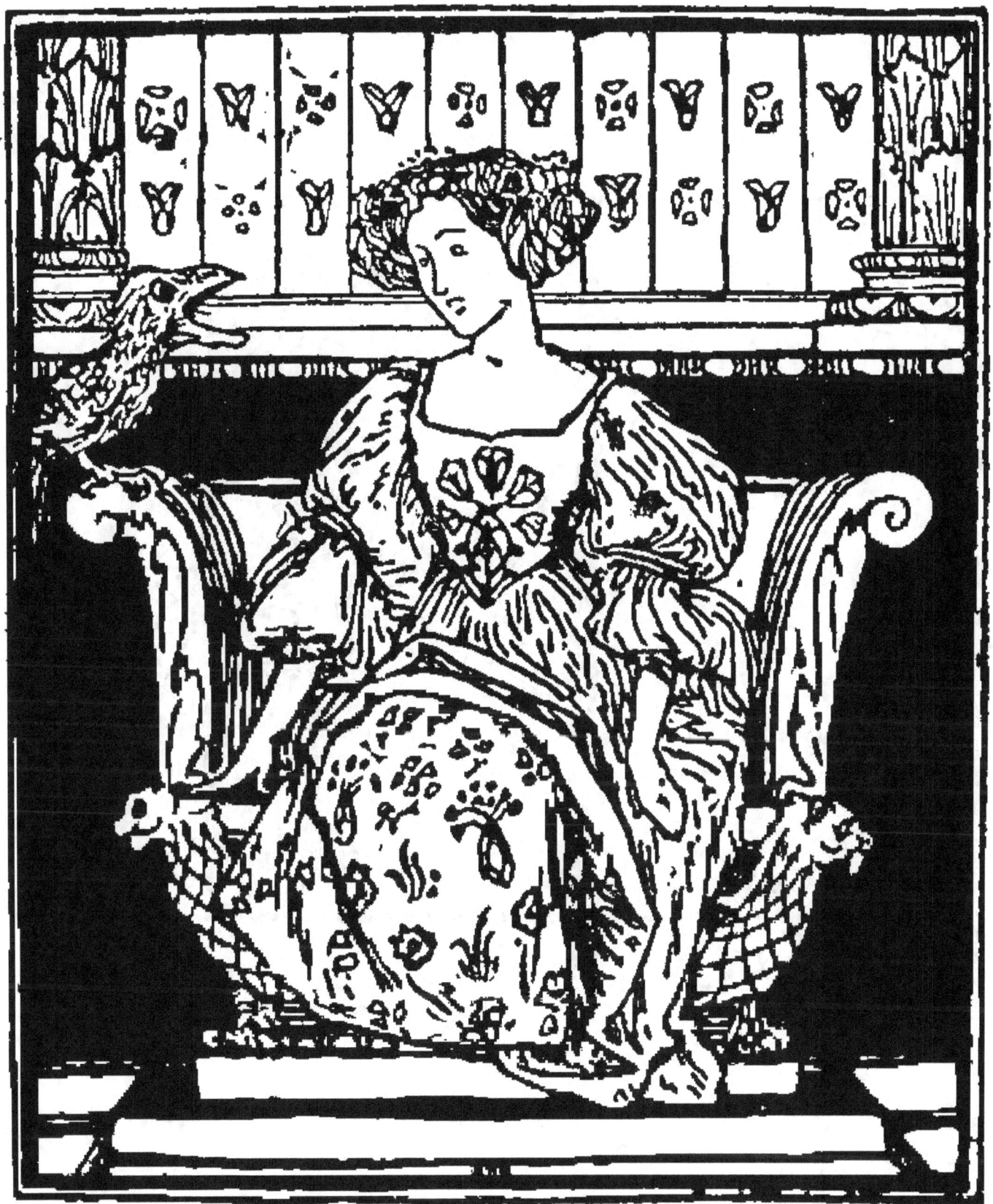

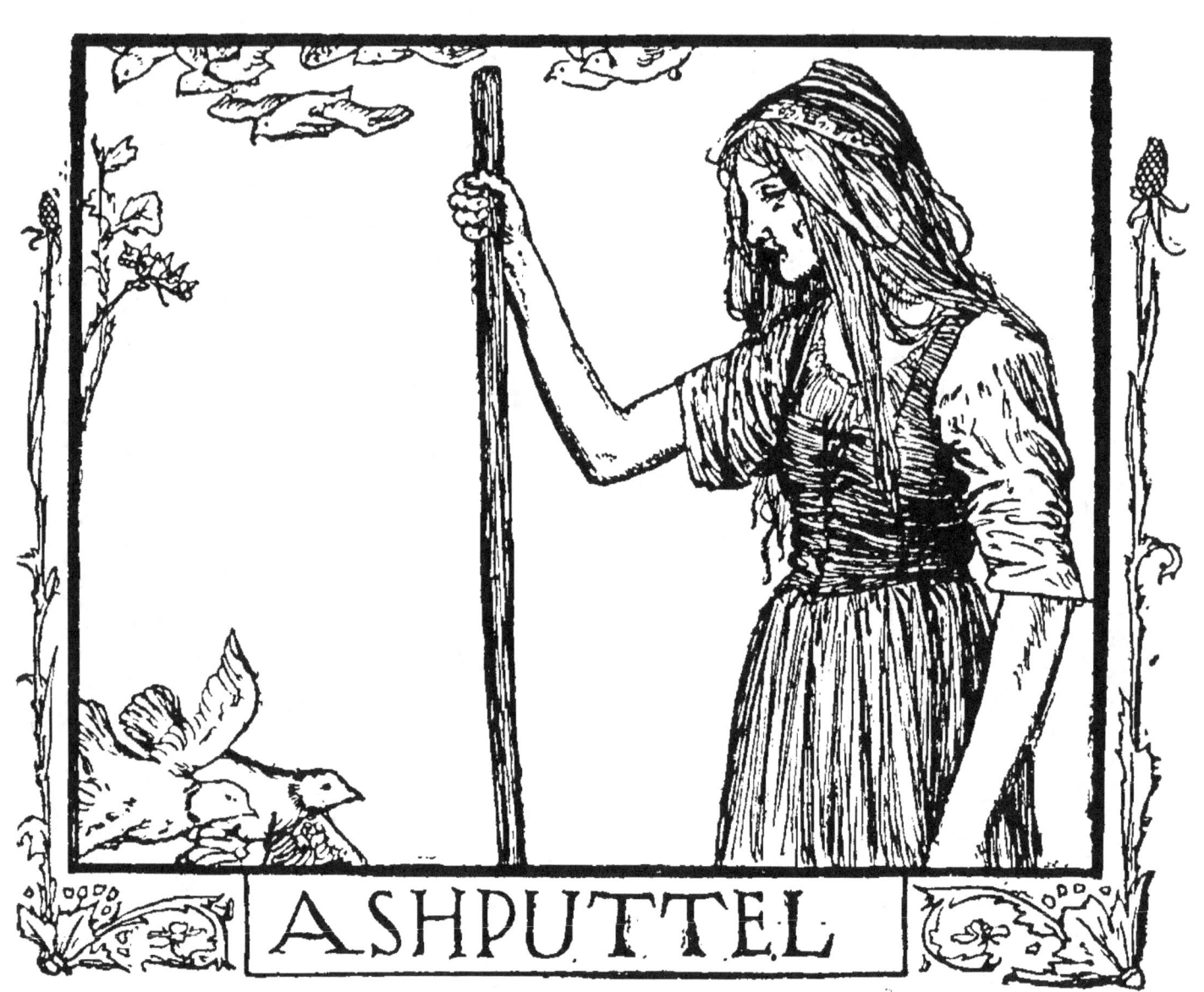

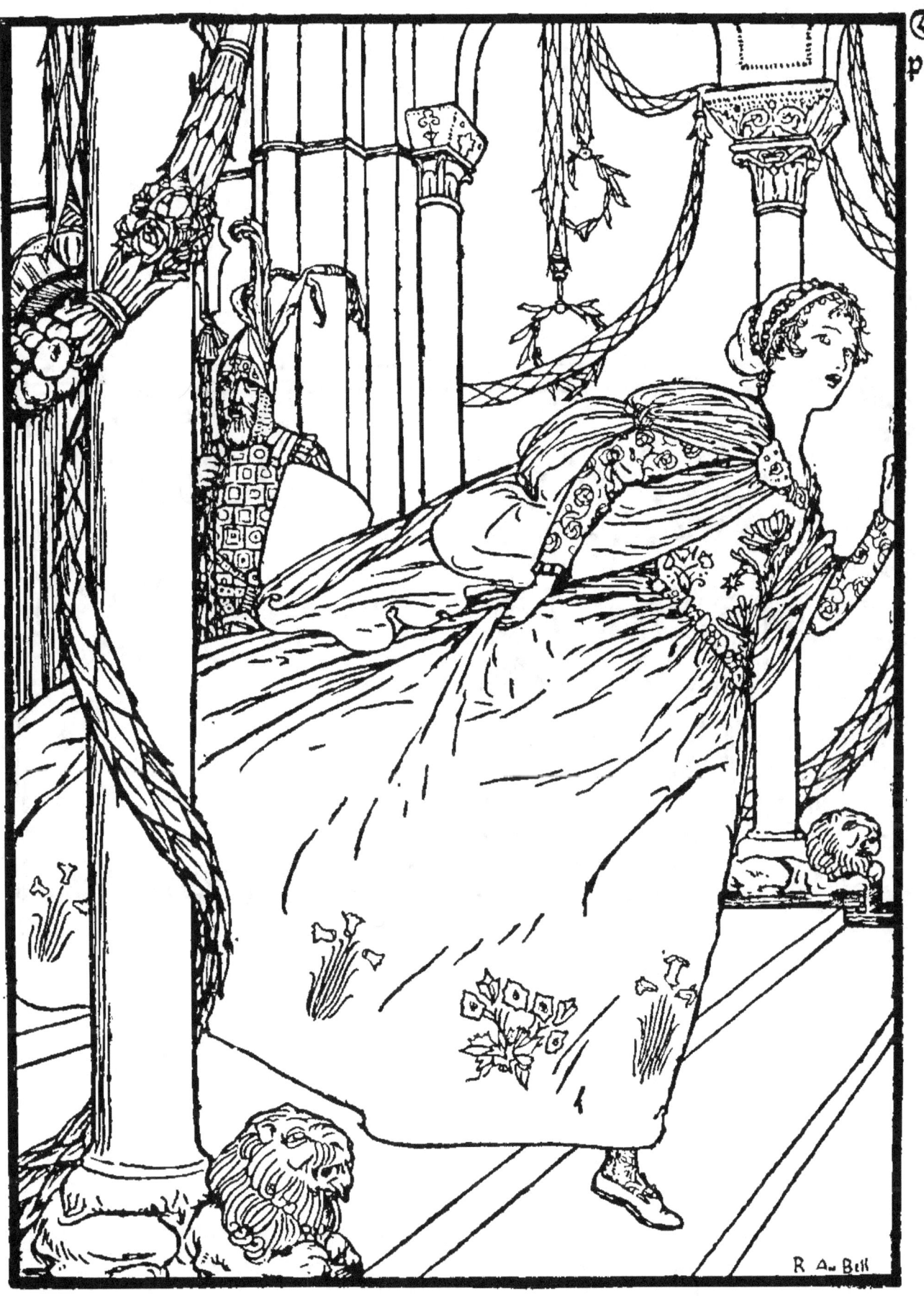

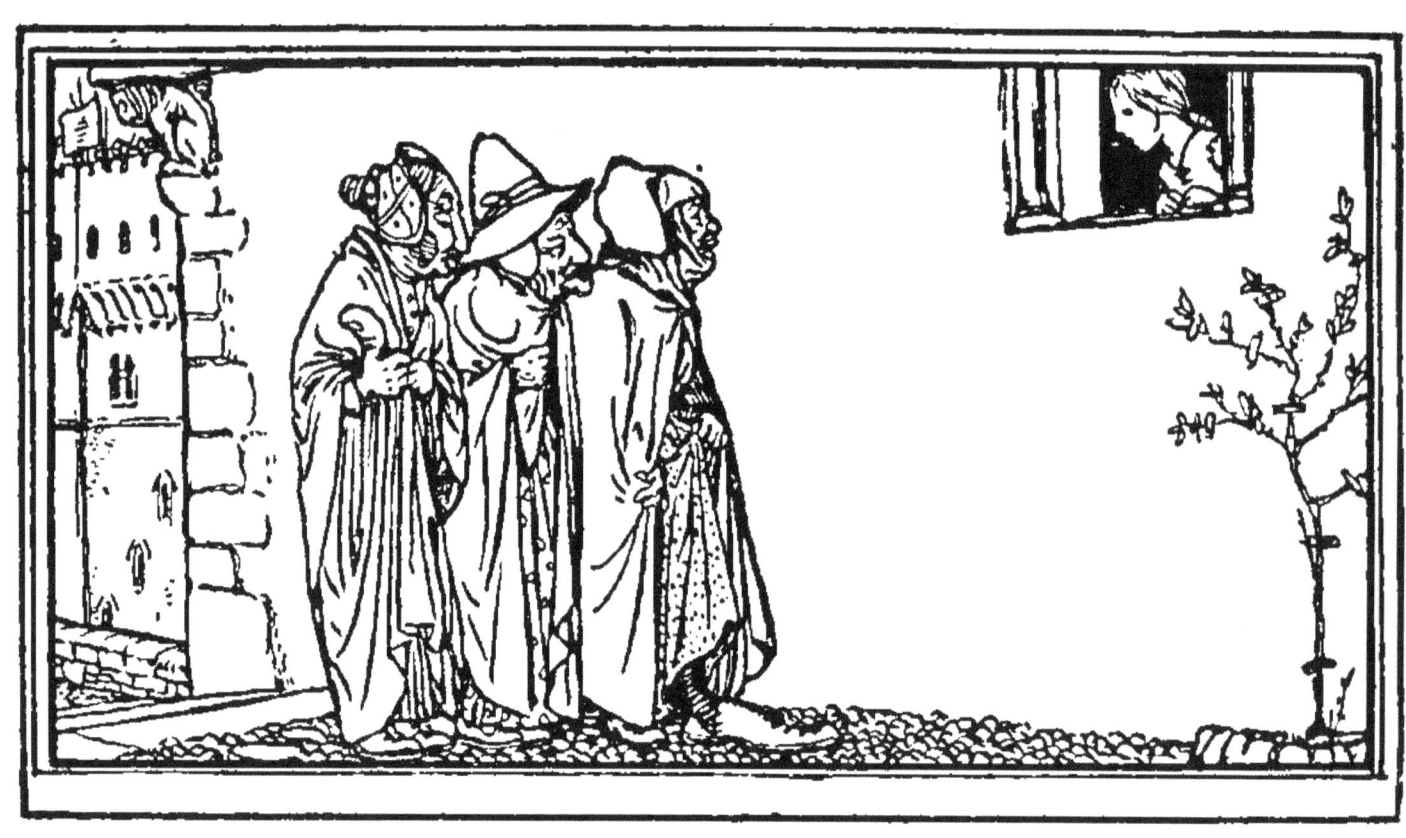

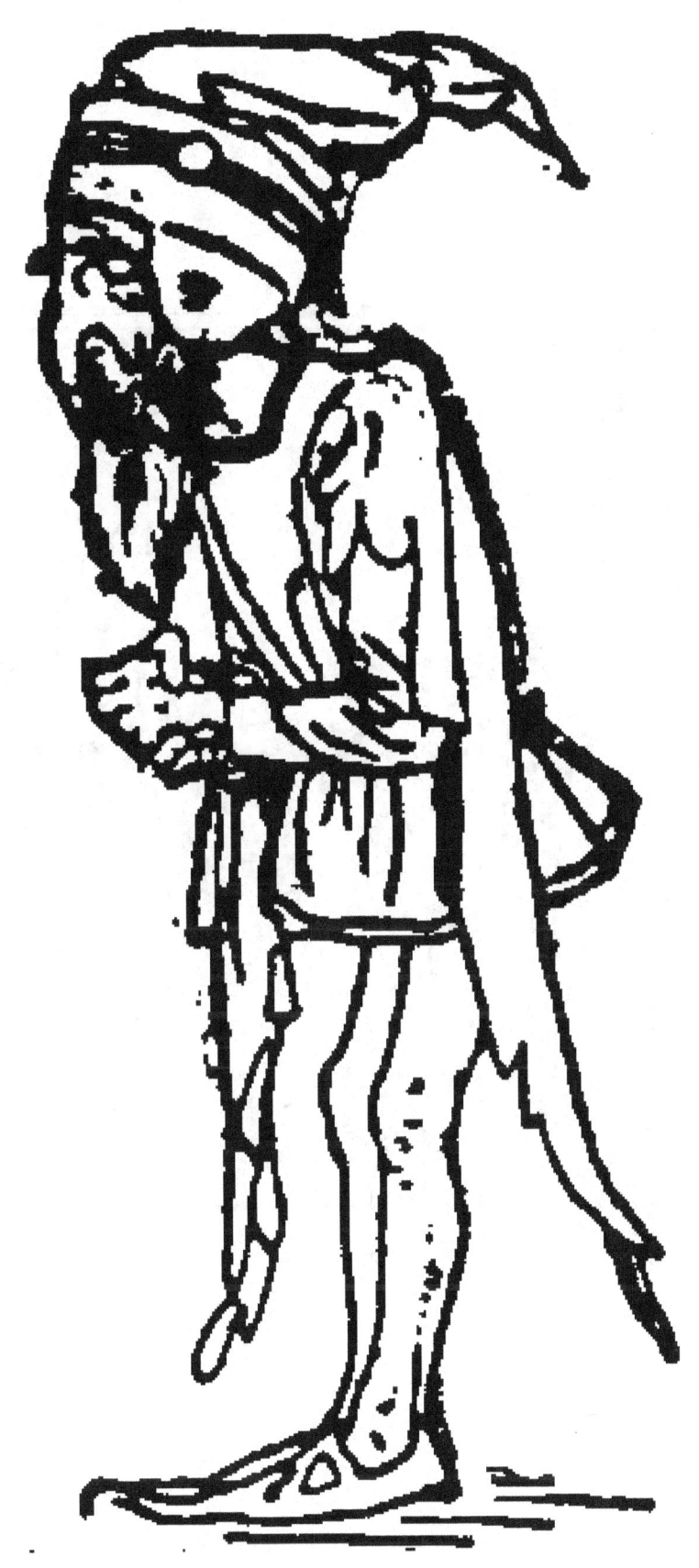

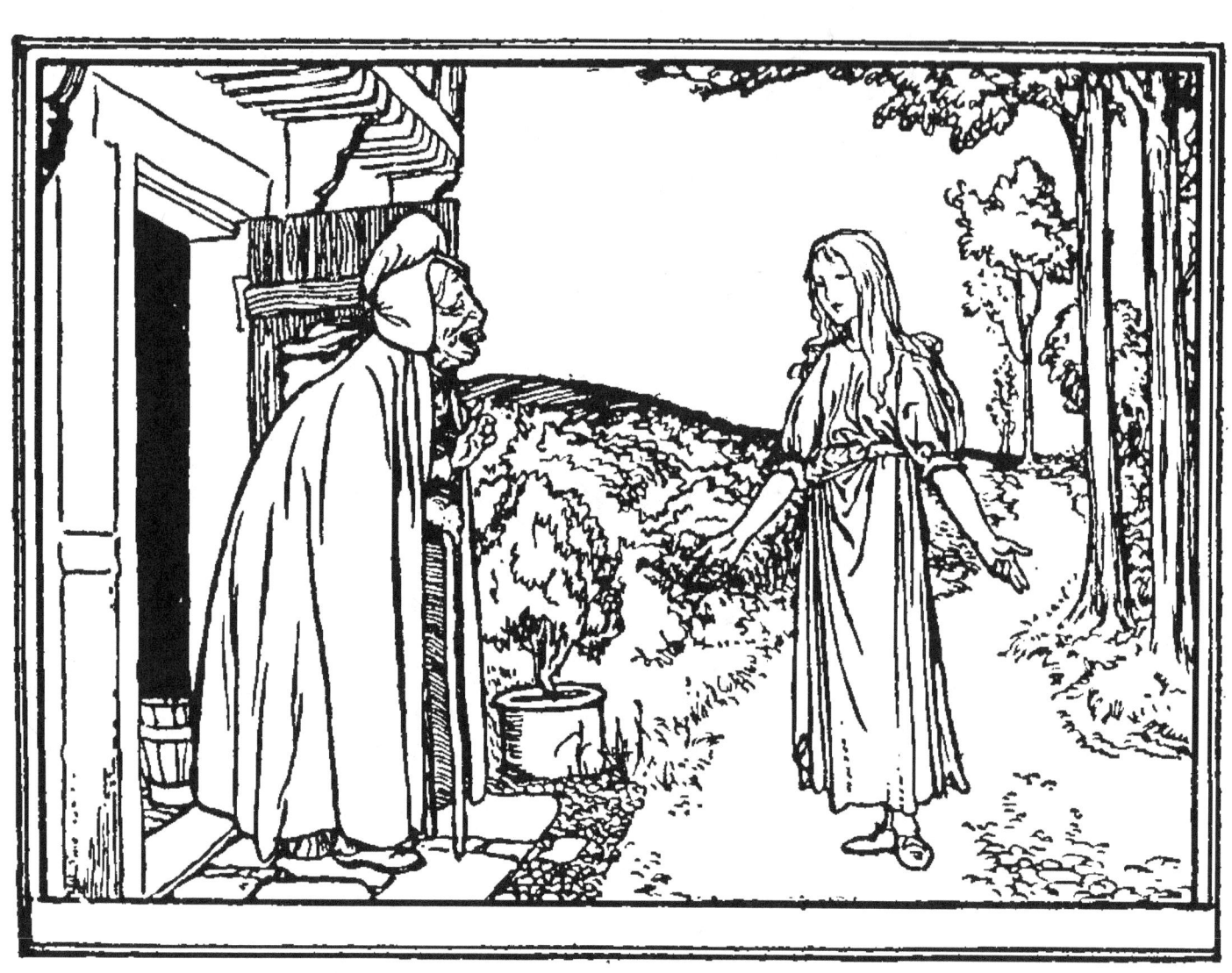

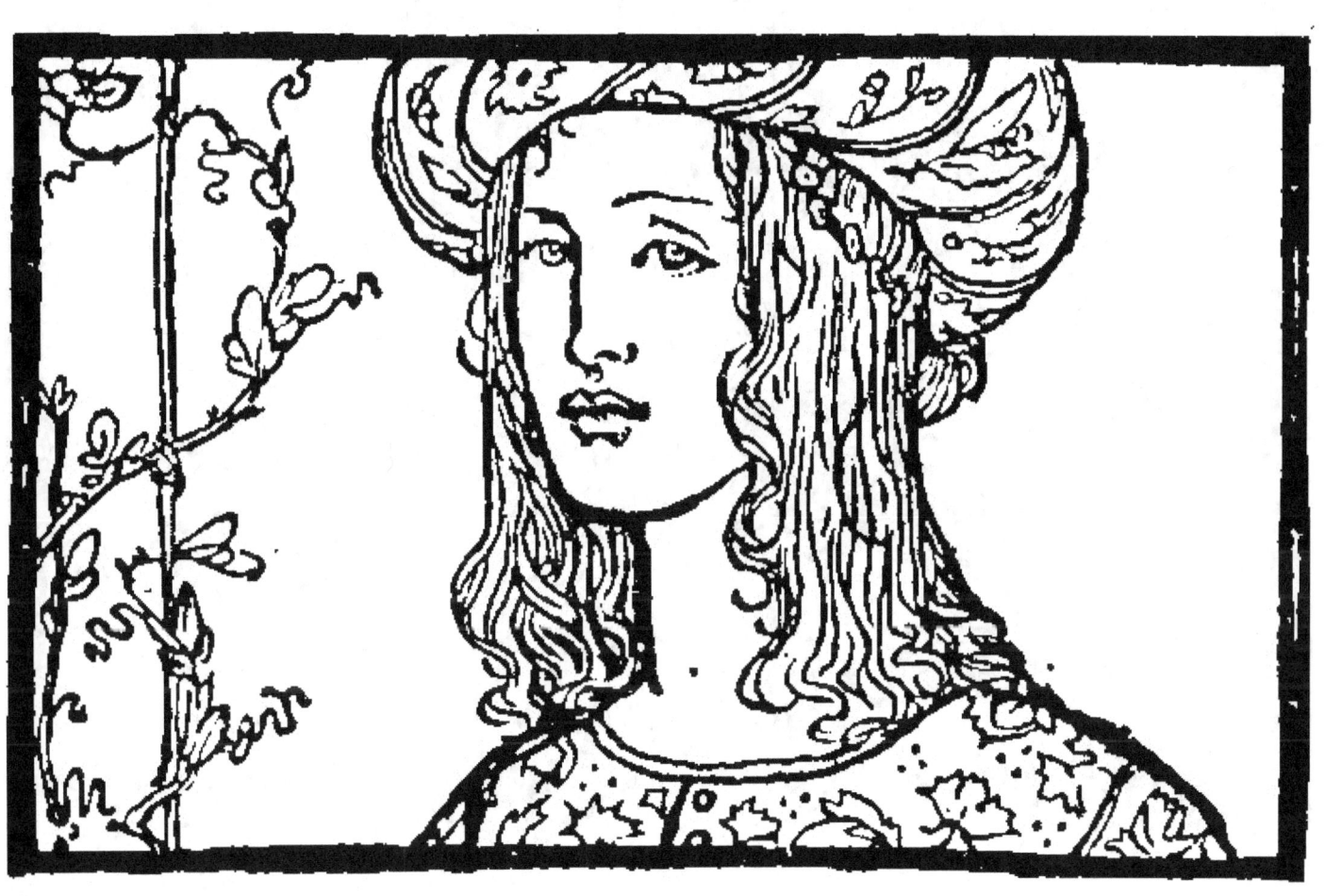

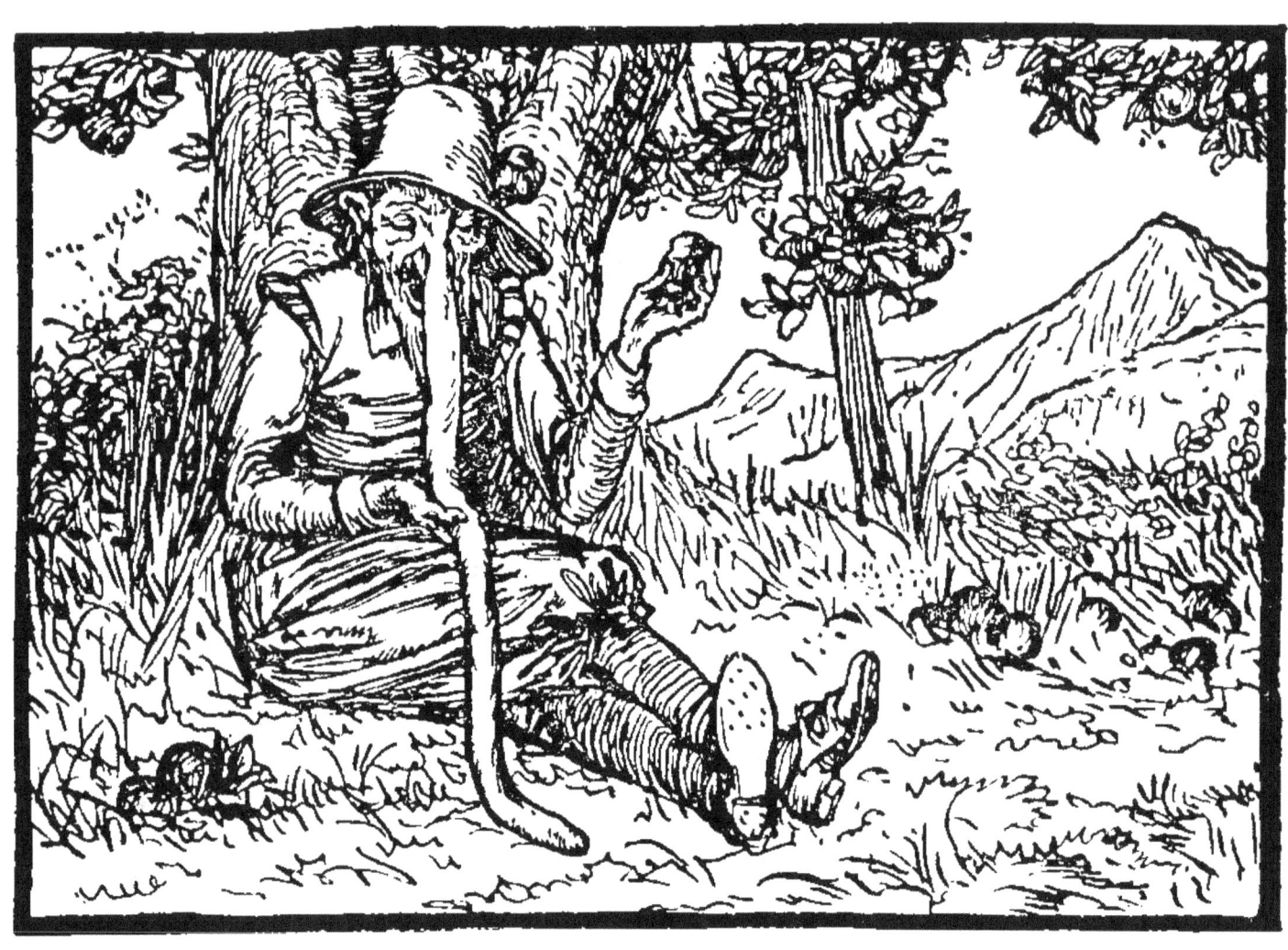

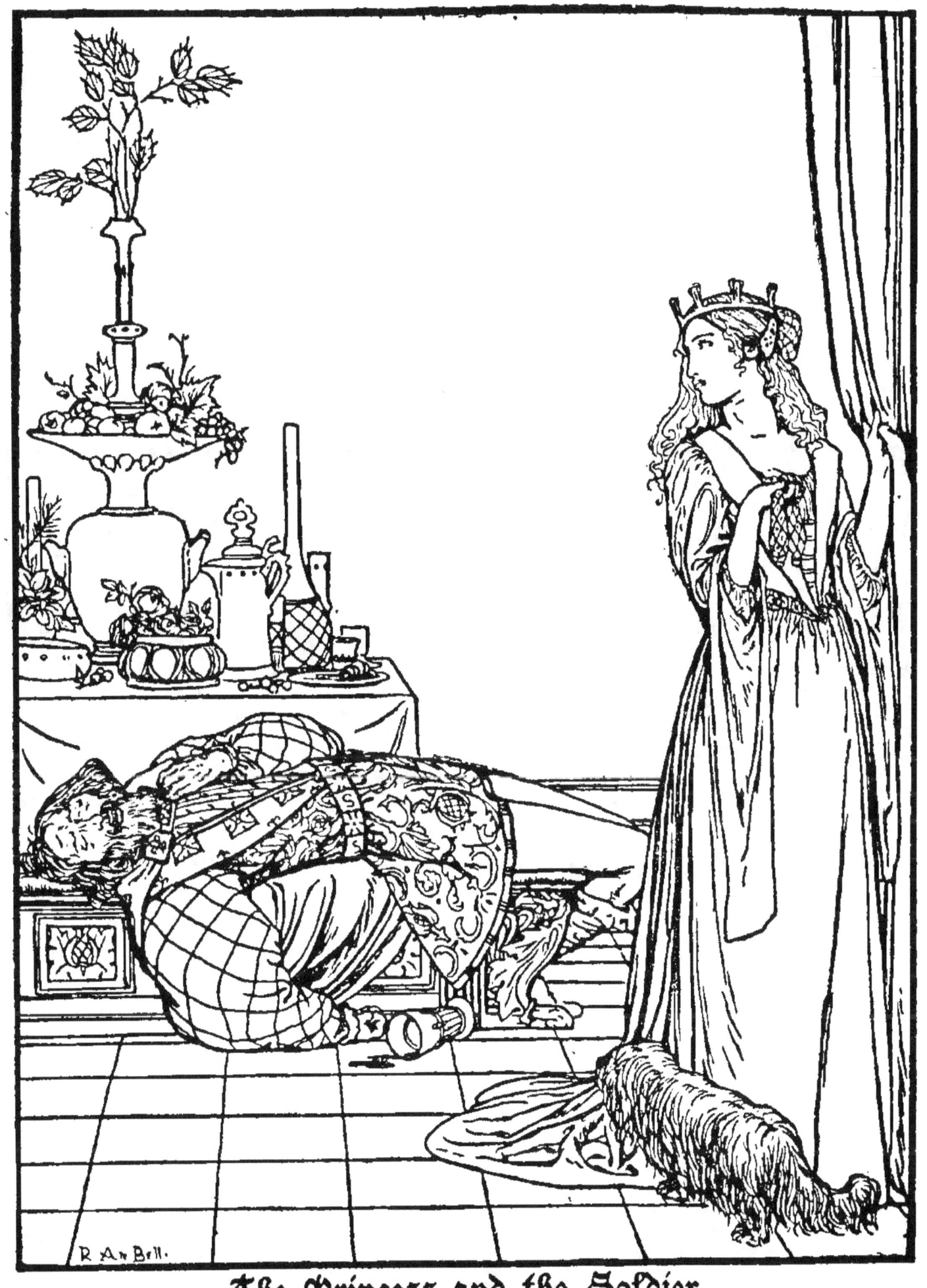

The Princess and the Soldier

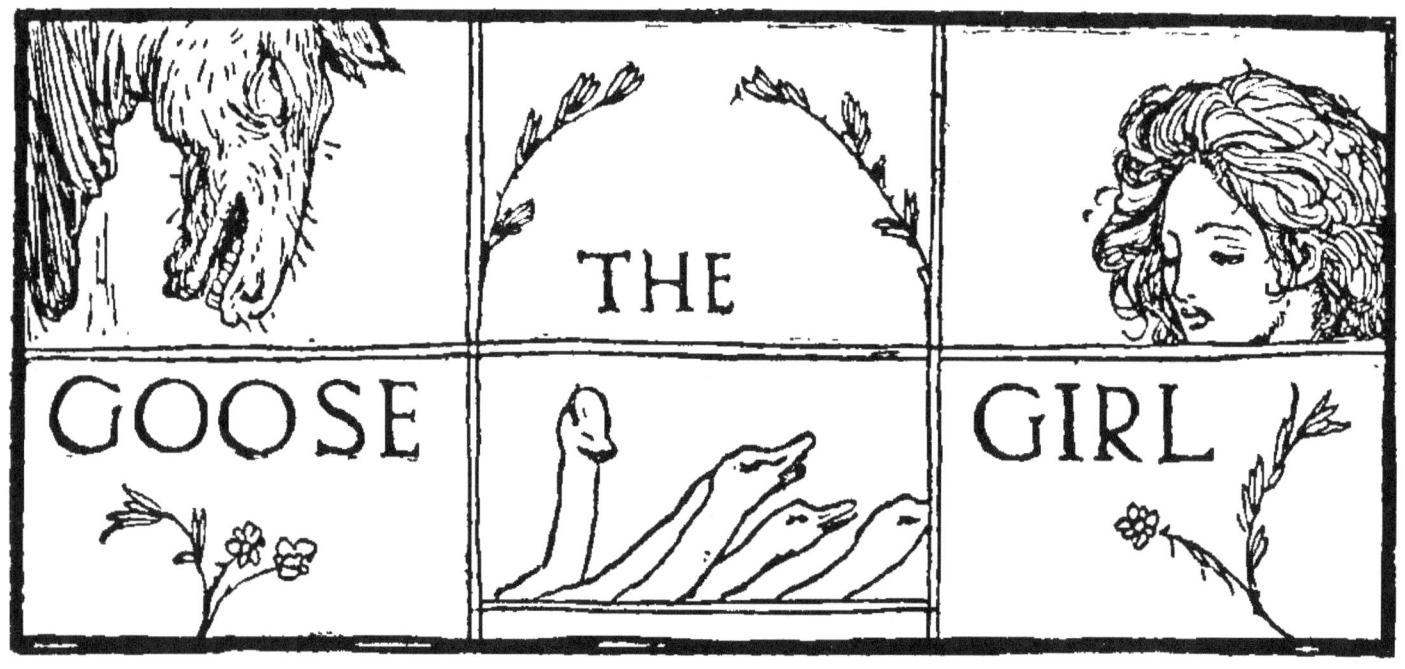

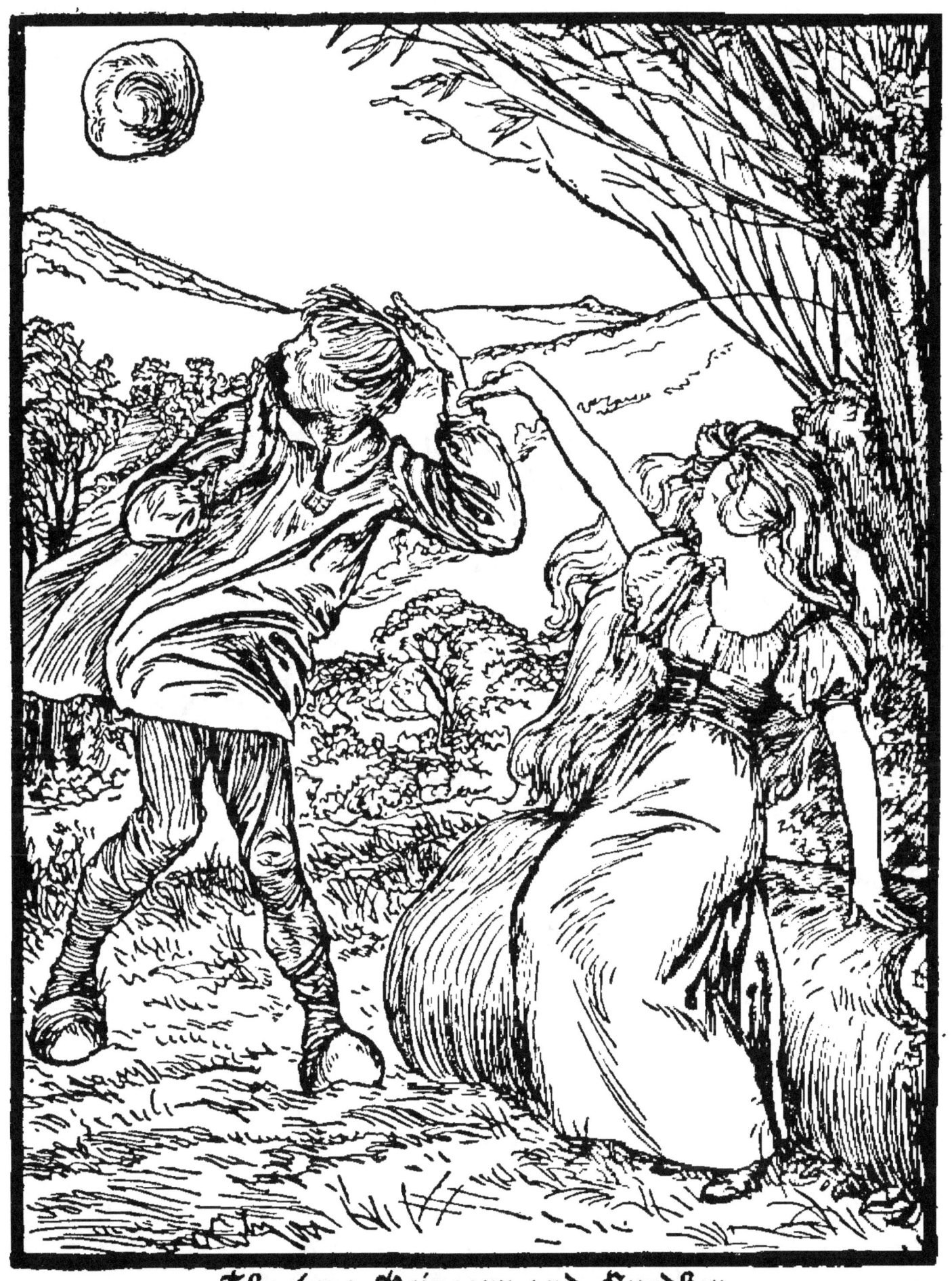

The true Princess and Curdken

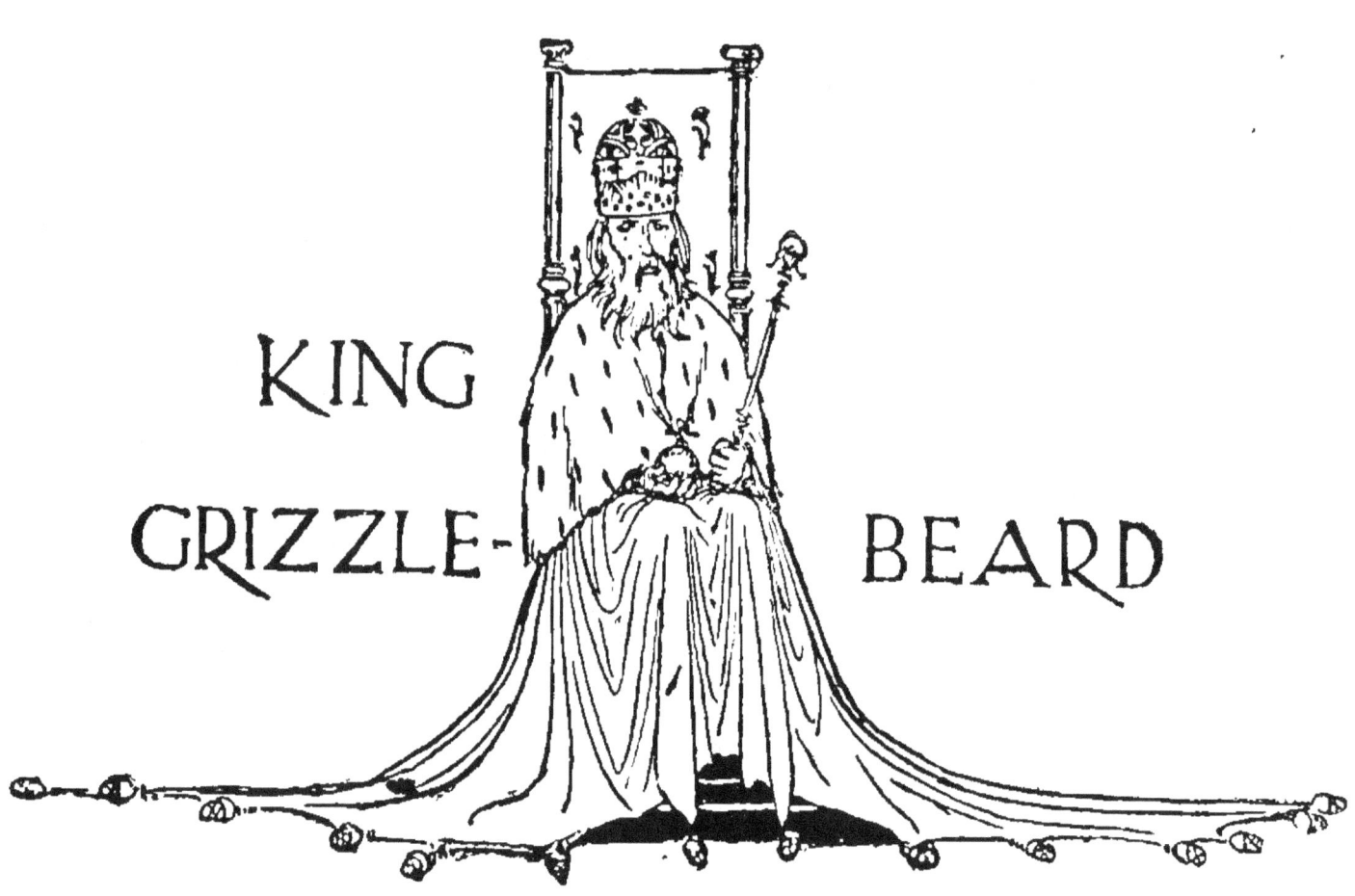

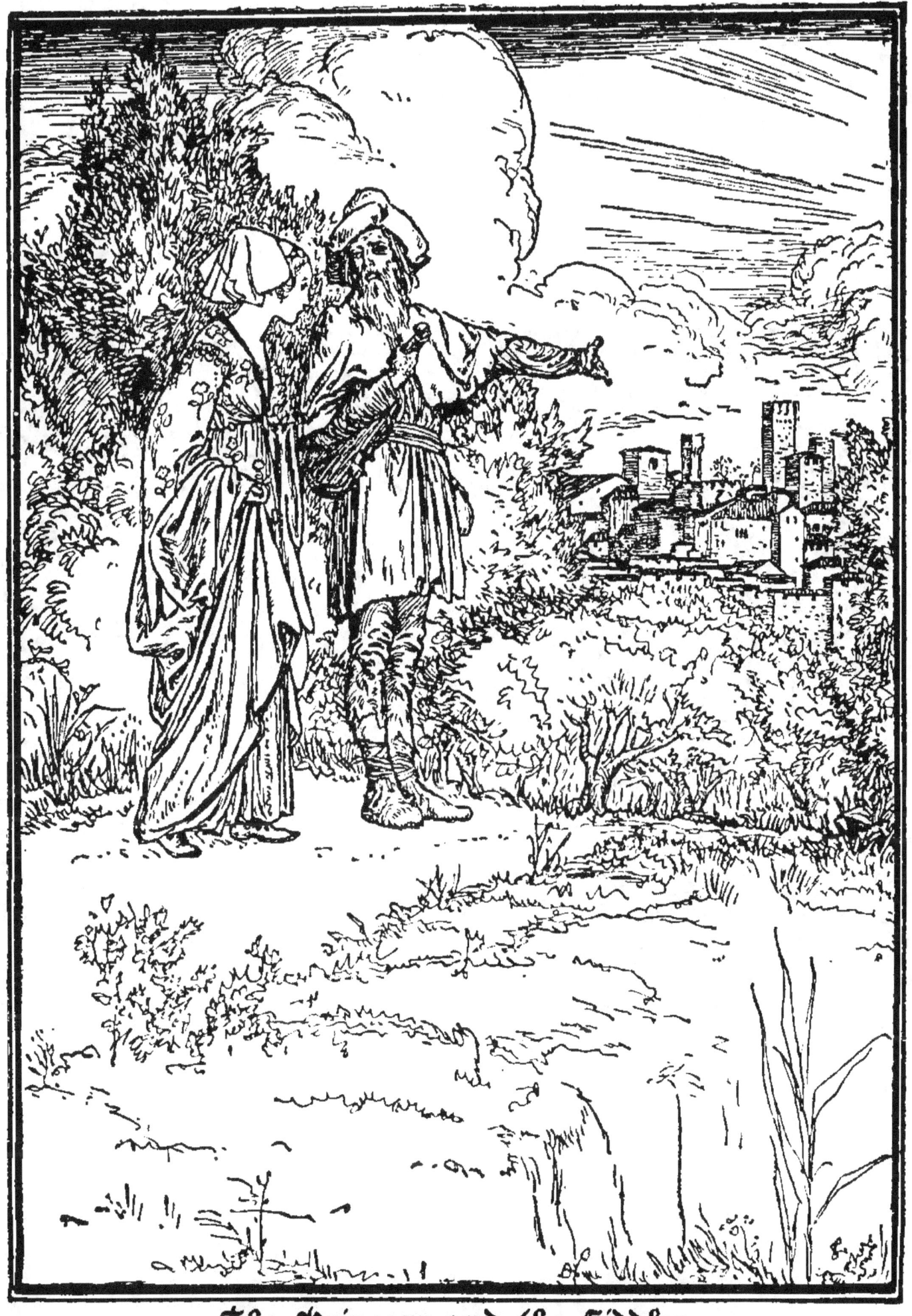
The Princess and the Fiddler

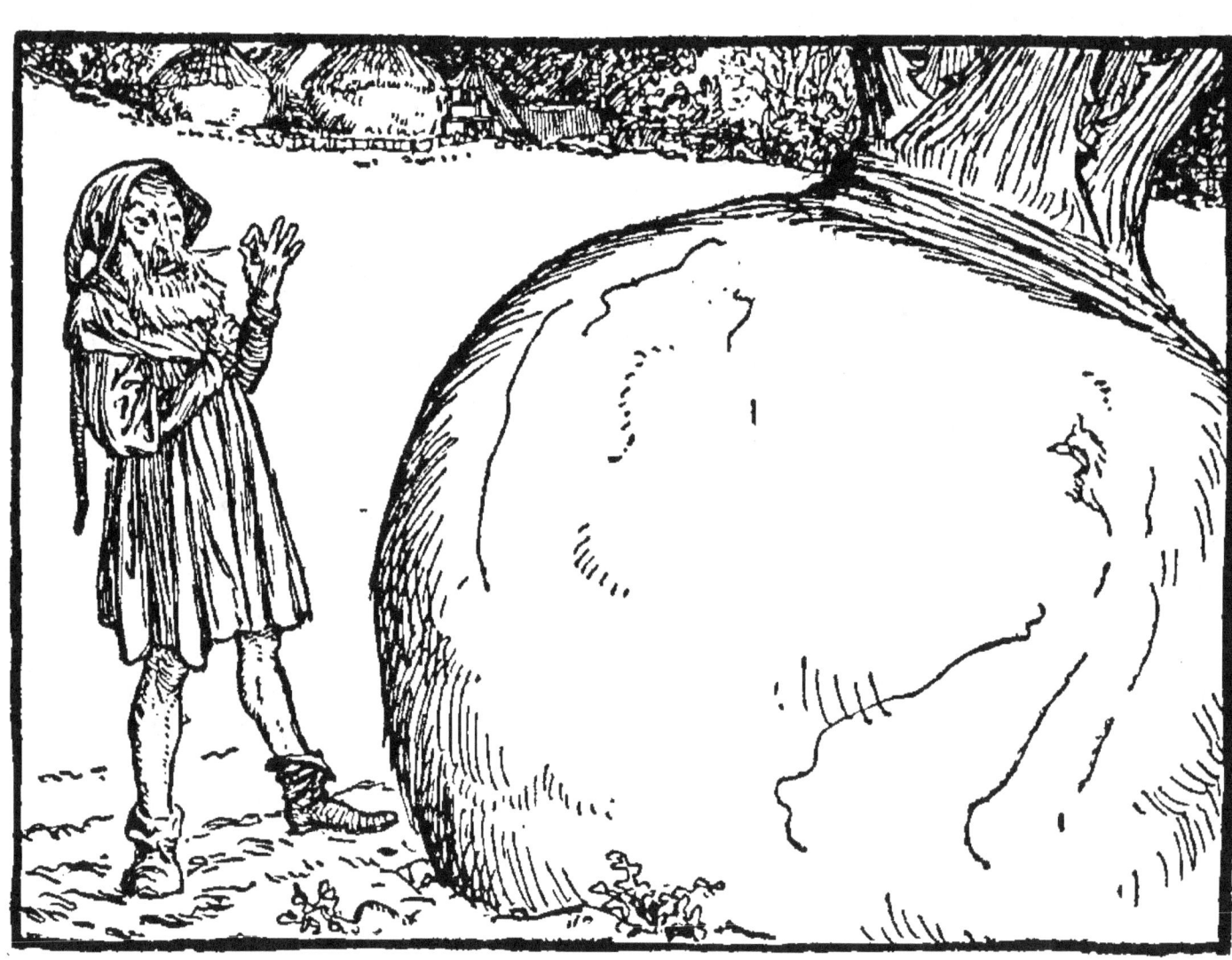

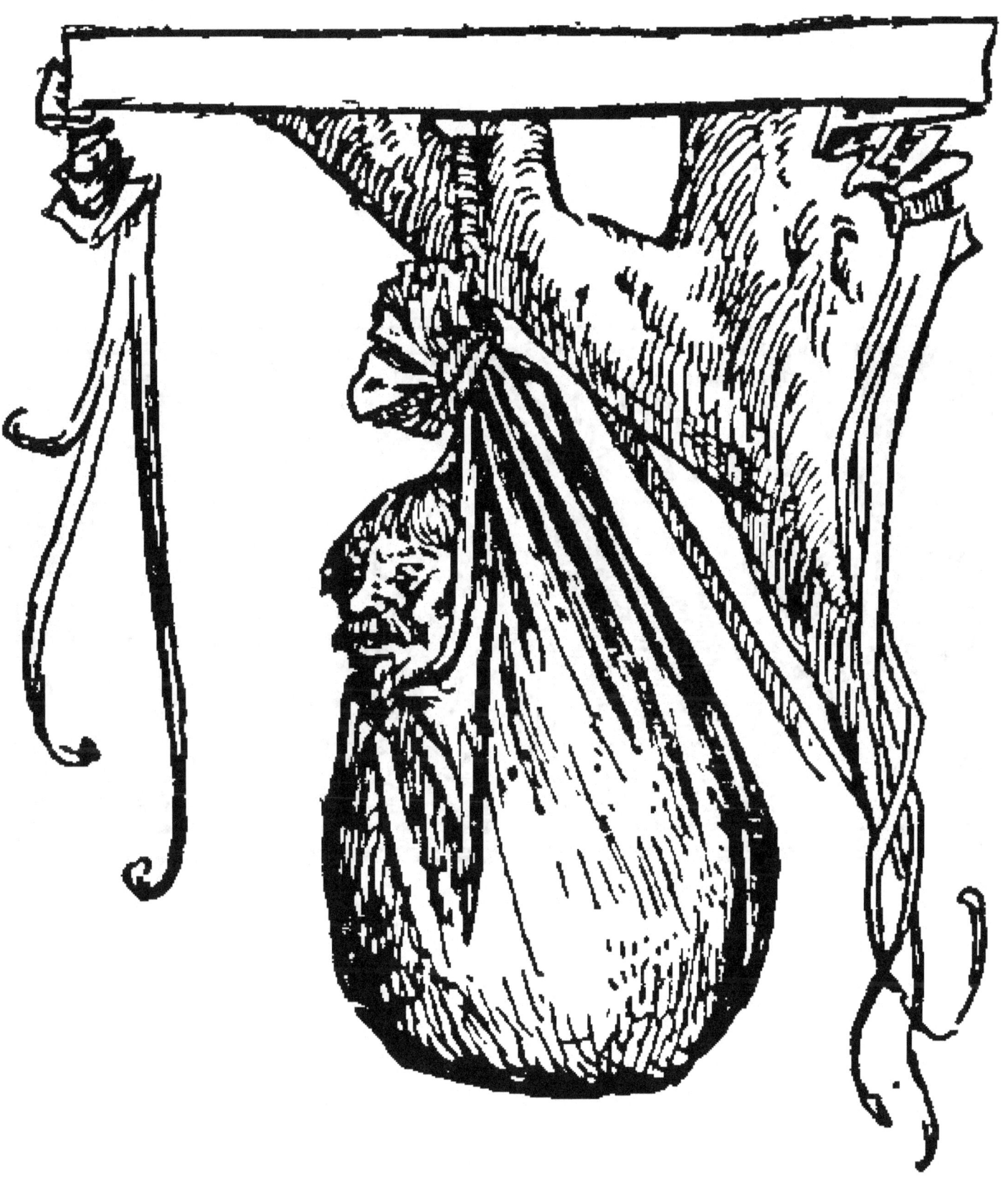

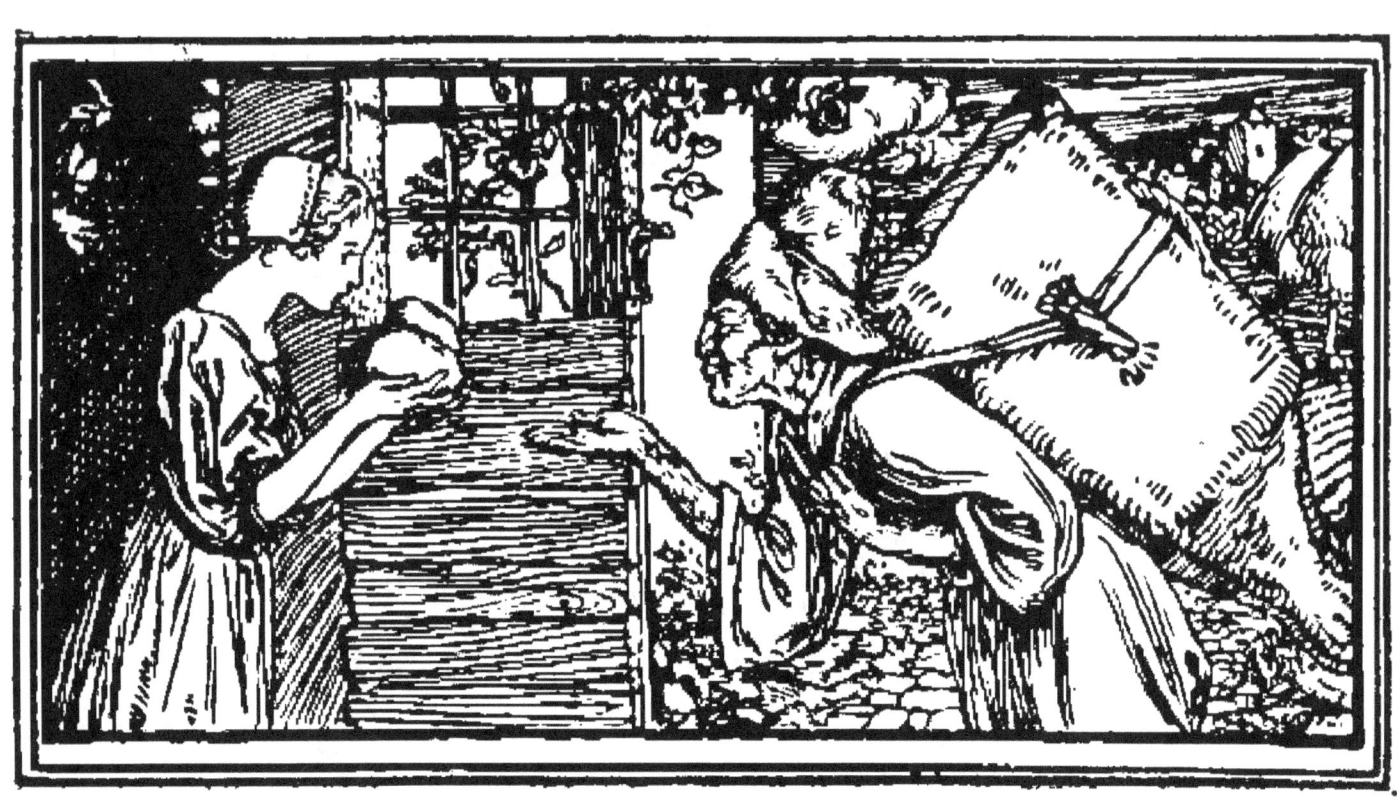

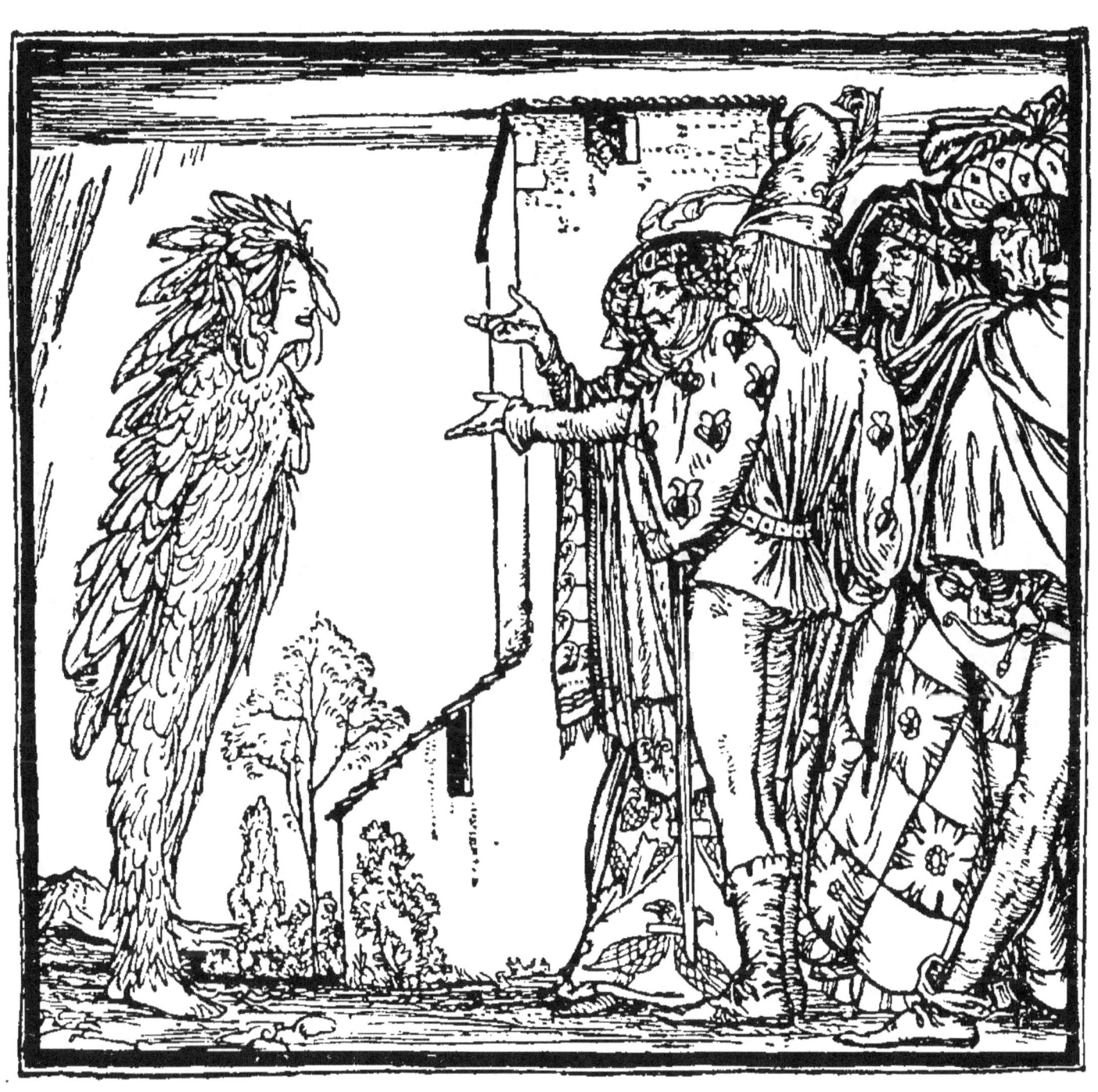

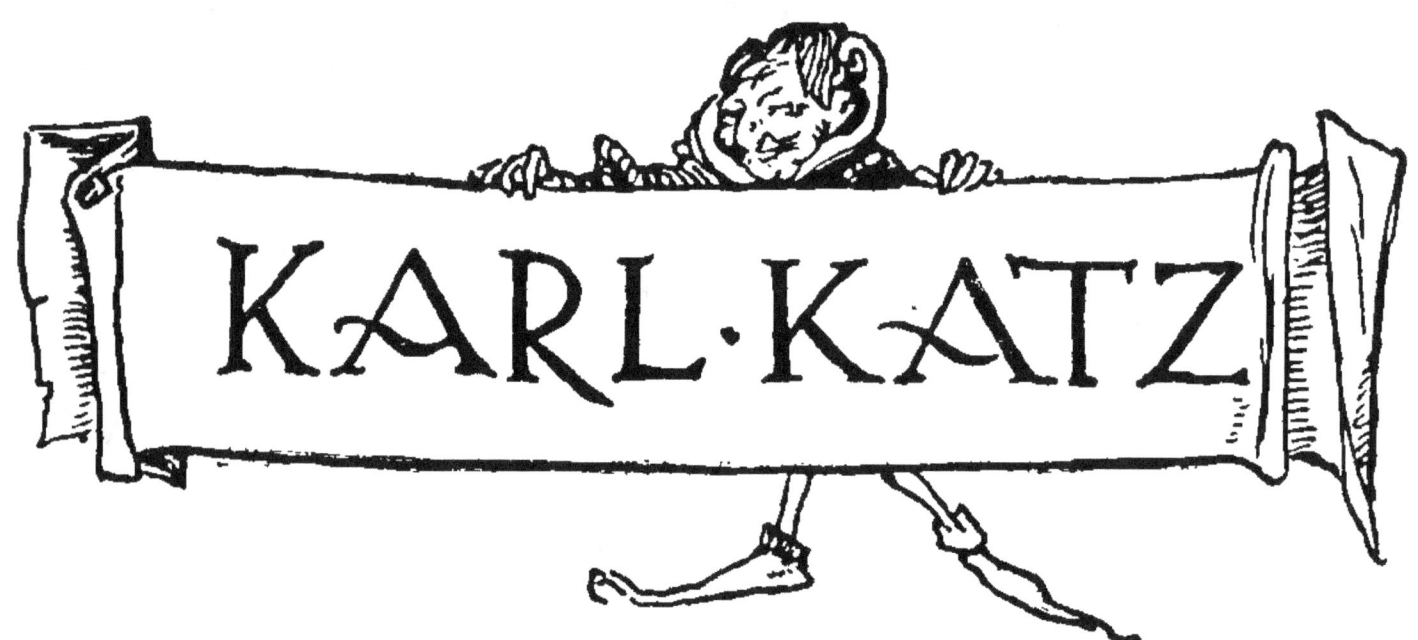

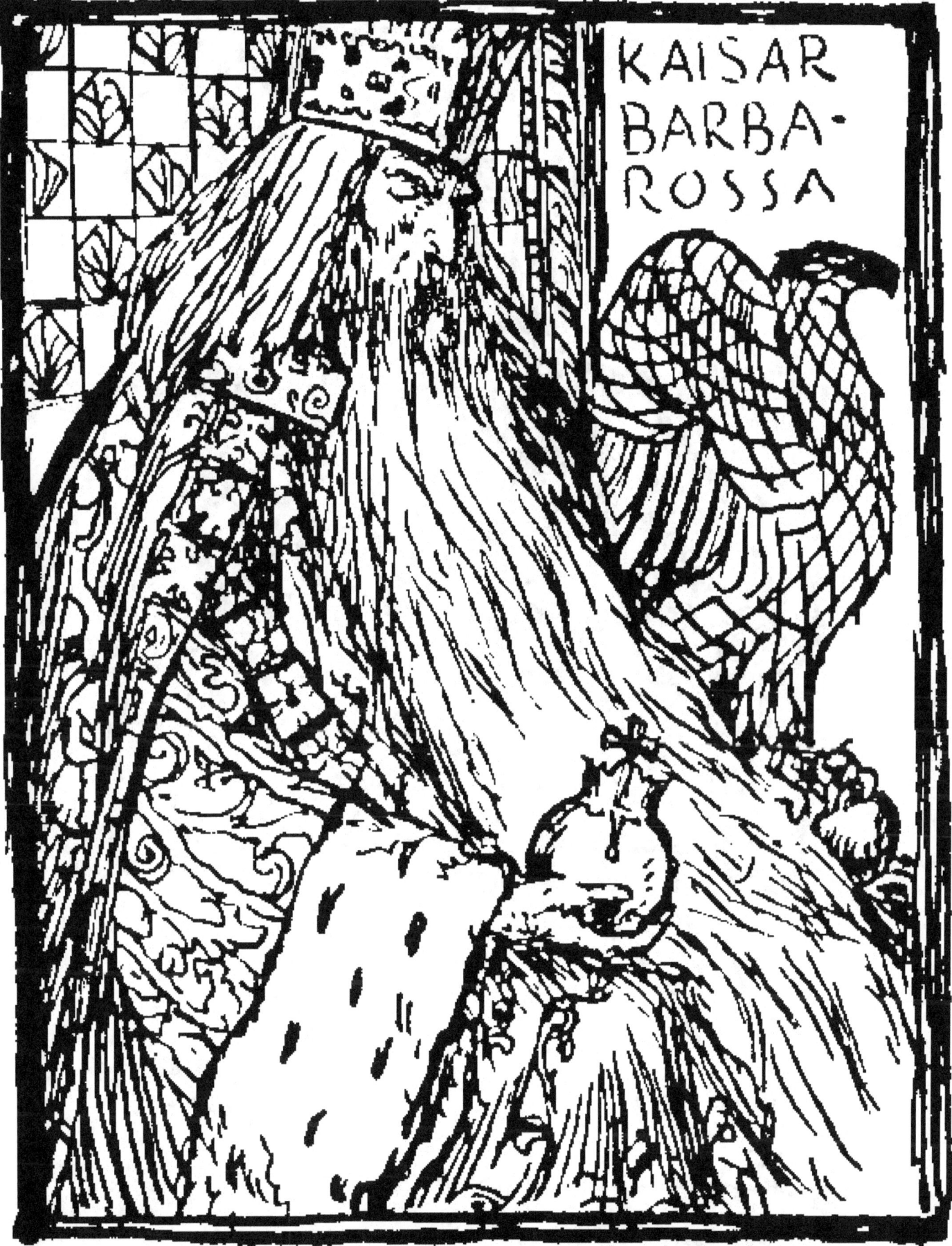

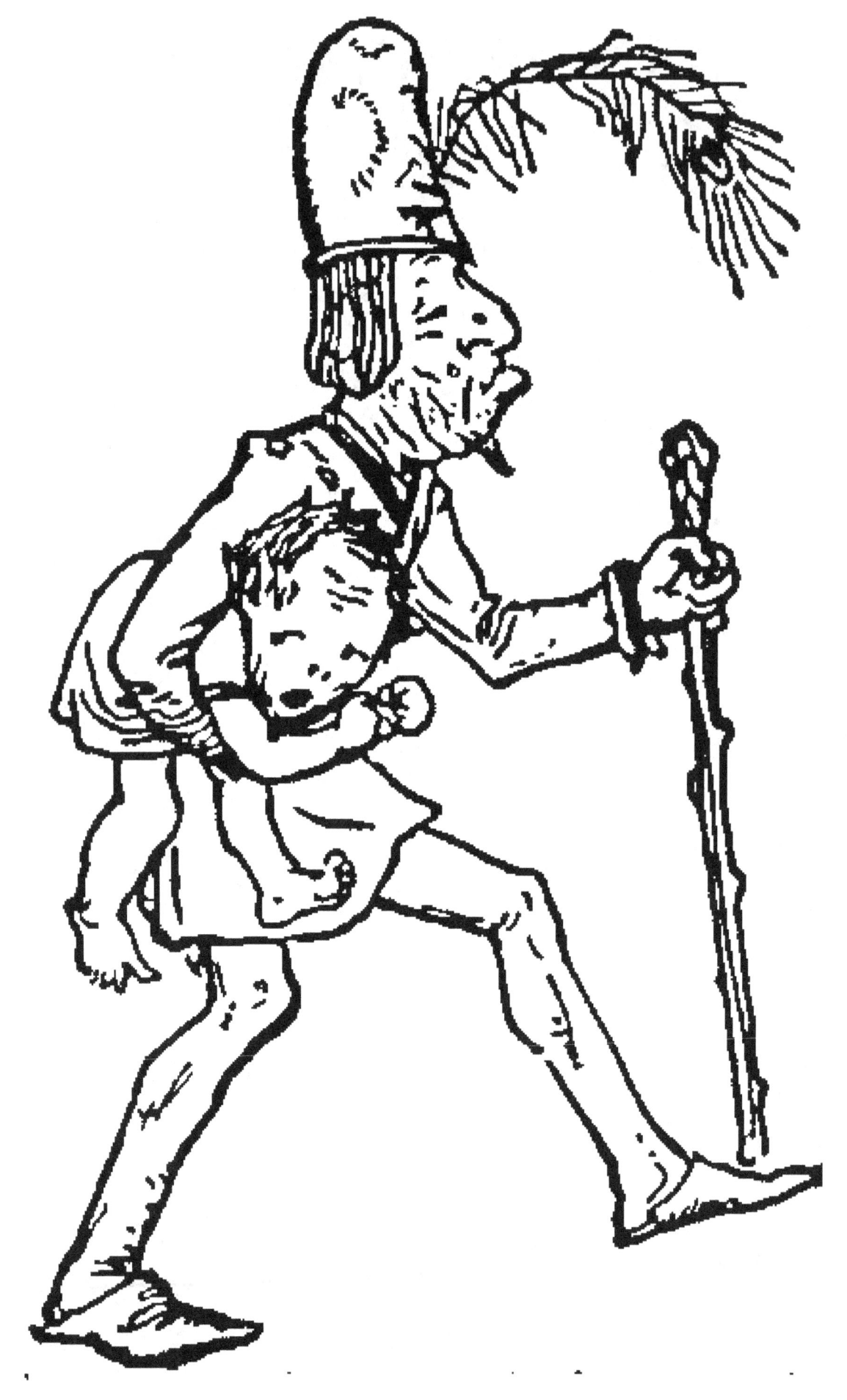

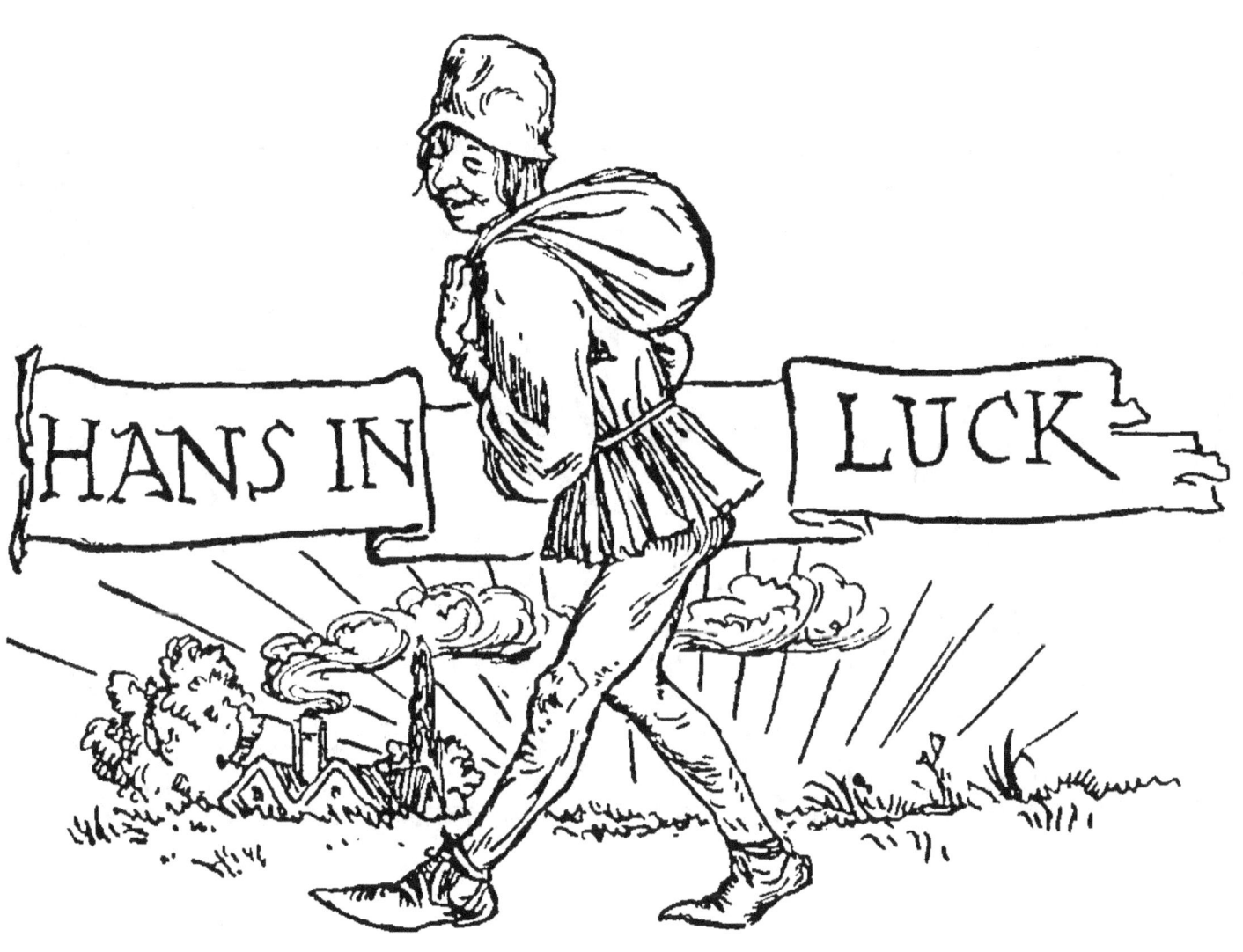

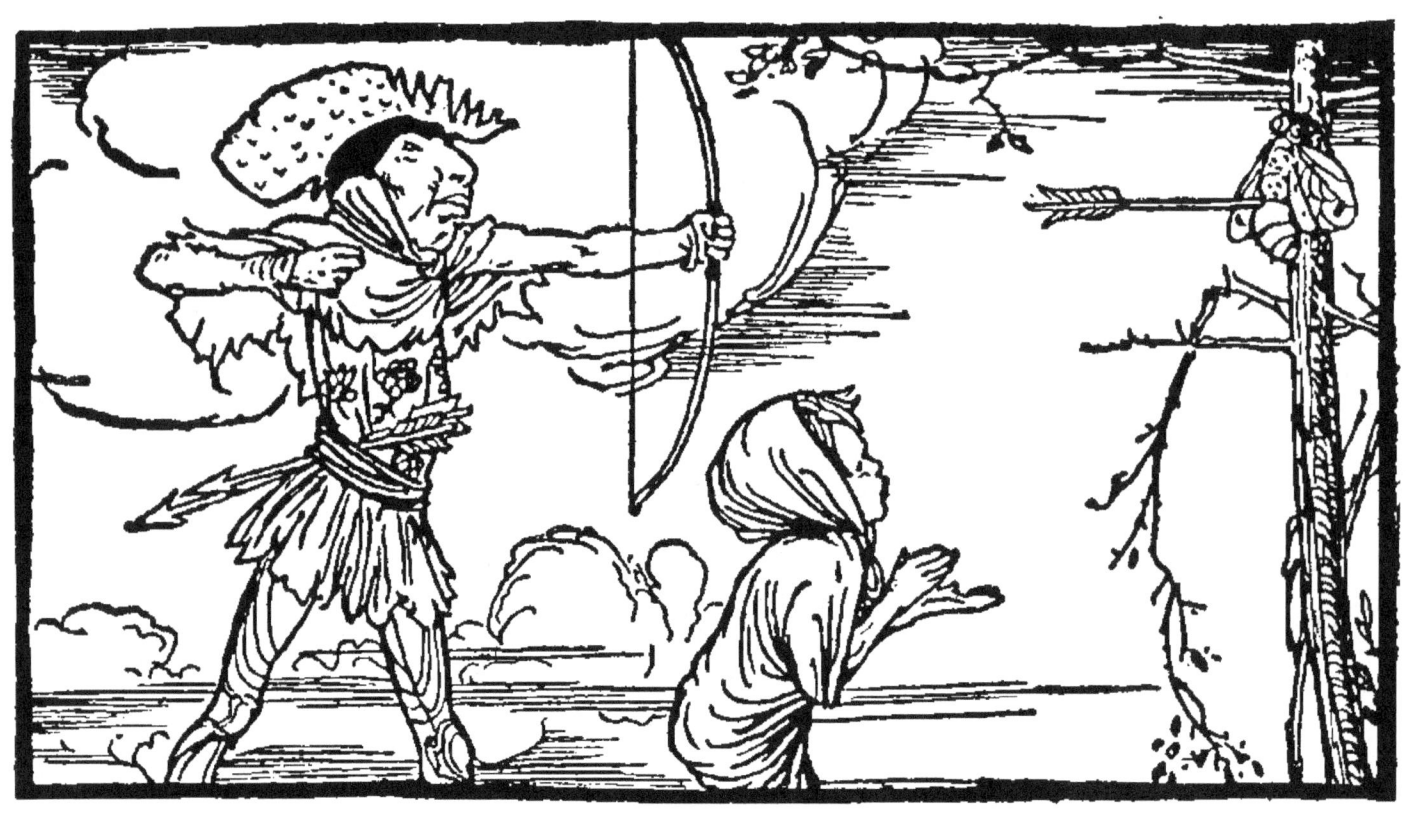

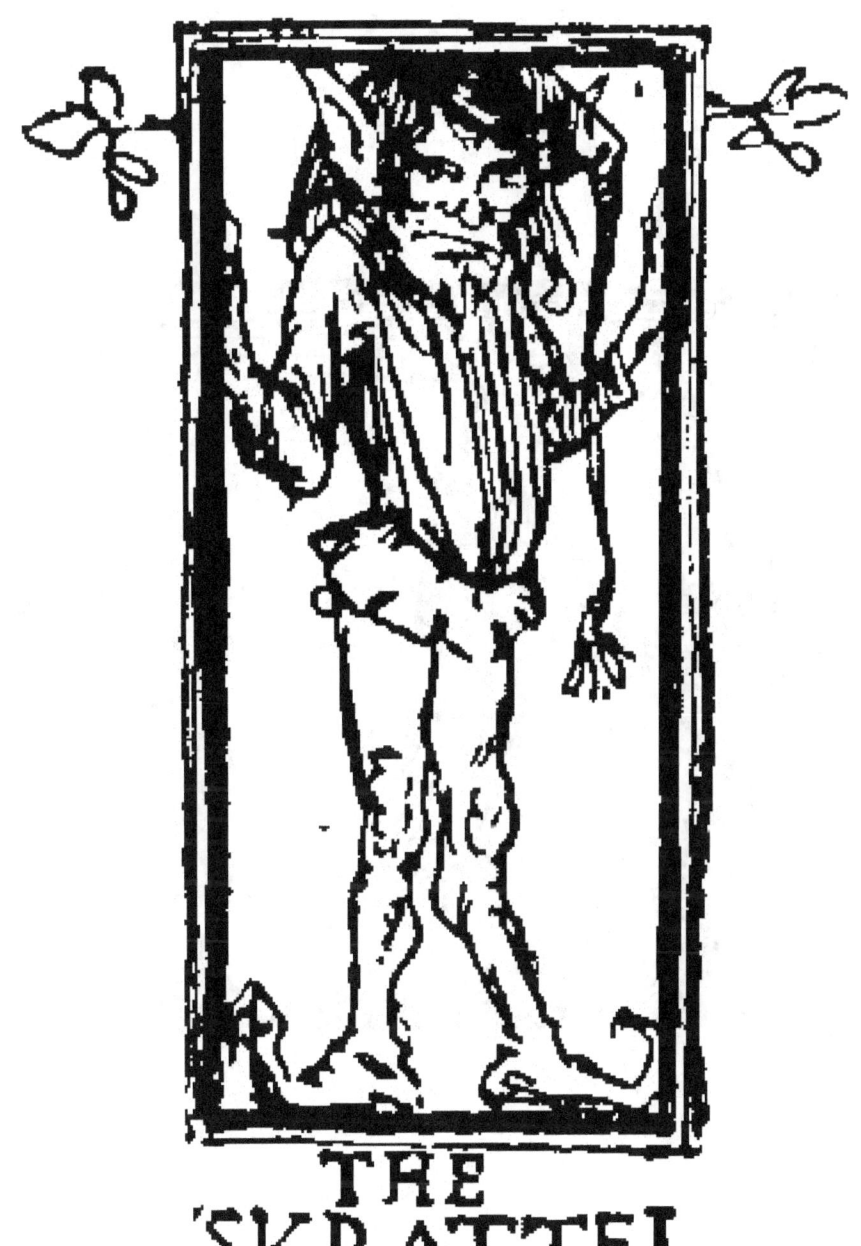

THE SKRATTEL

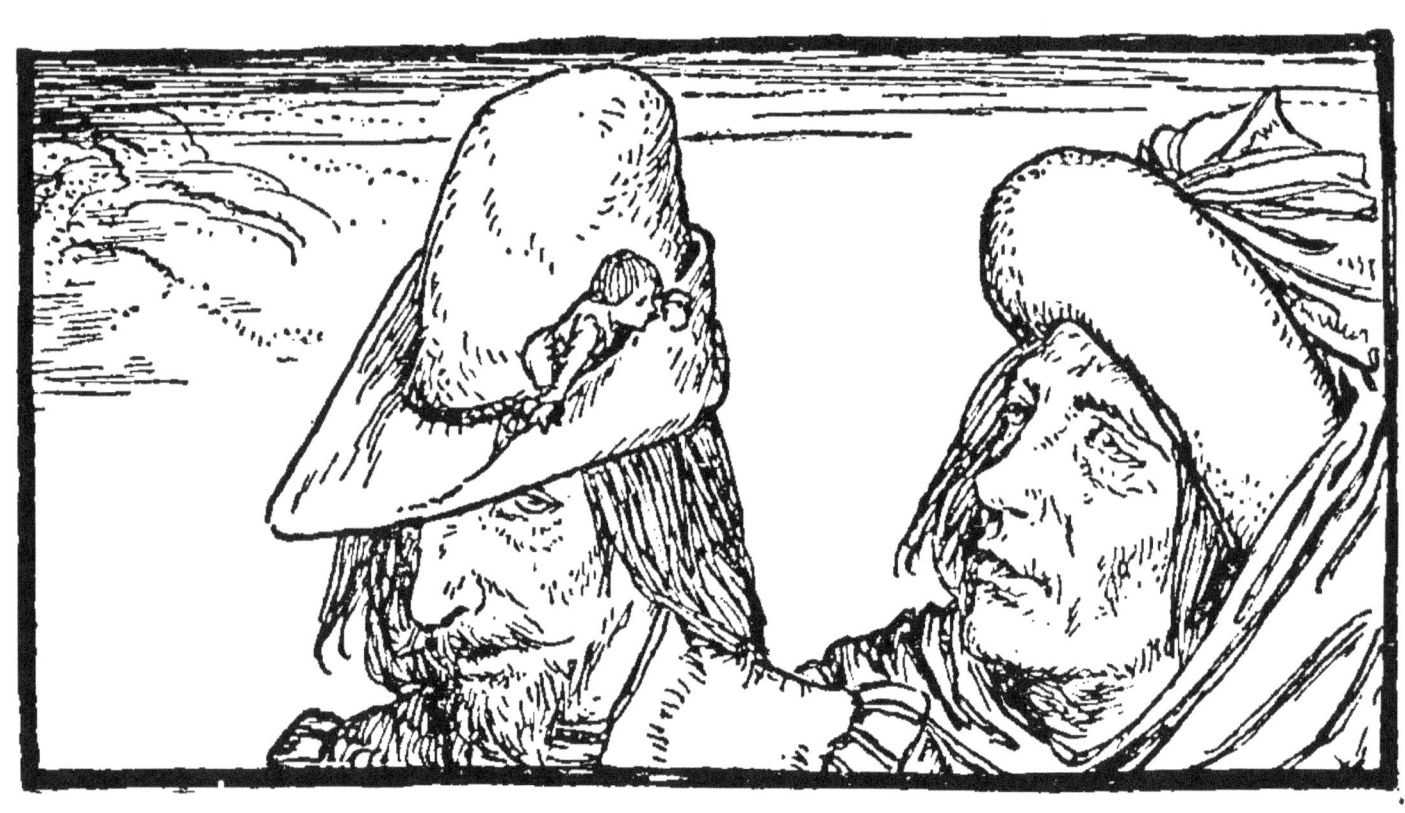

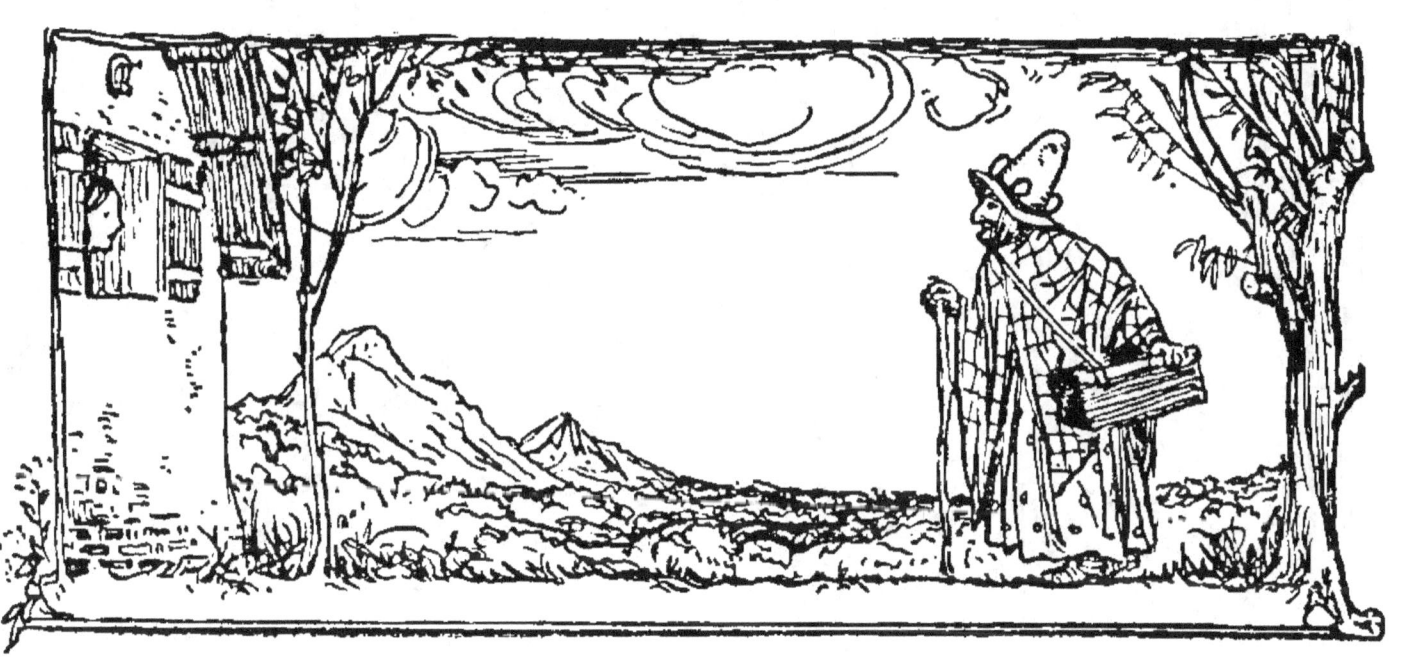

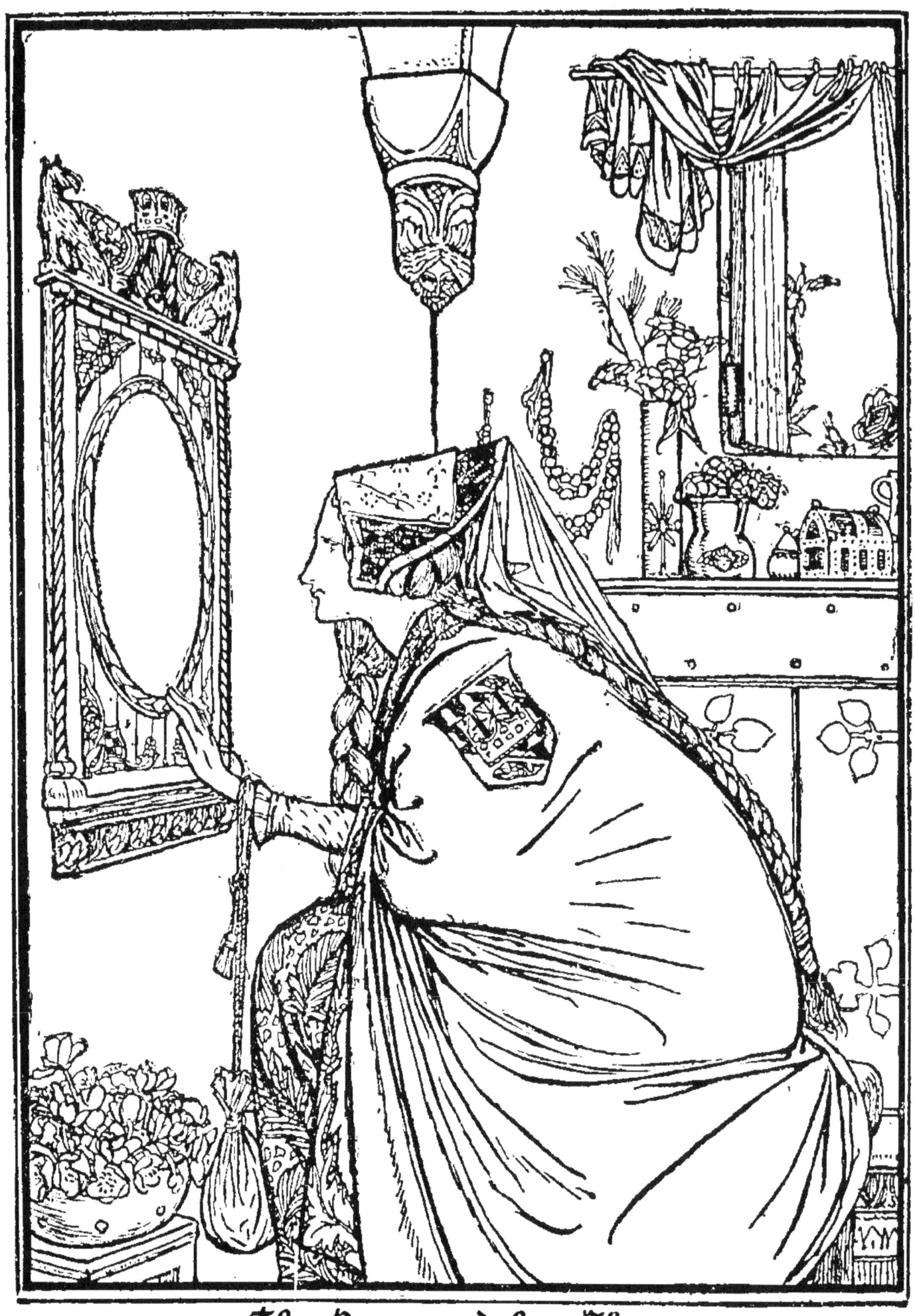

The Queen and her Glass

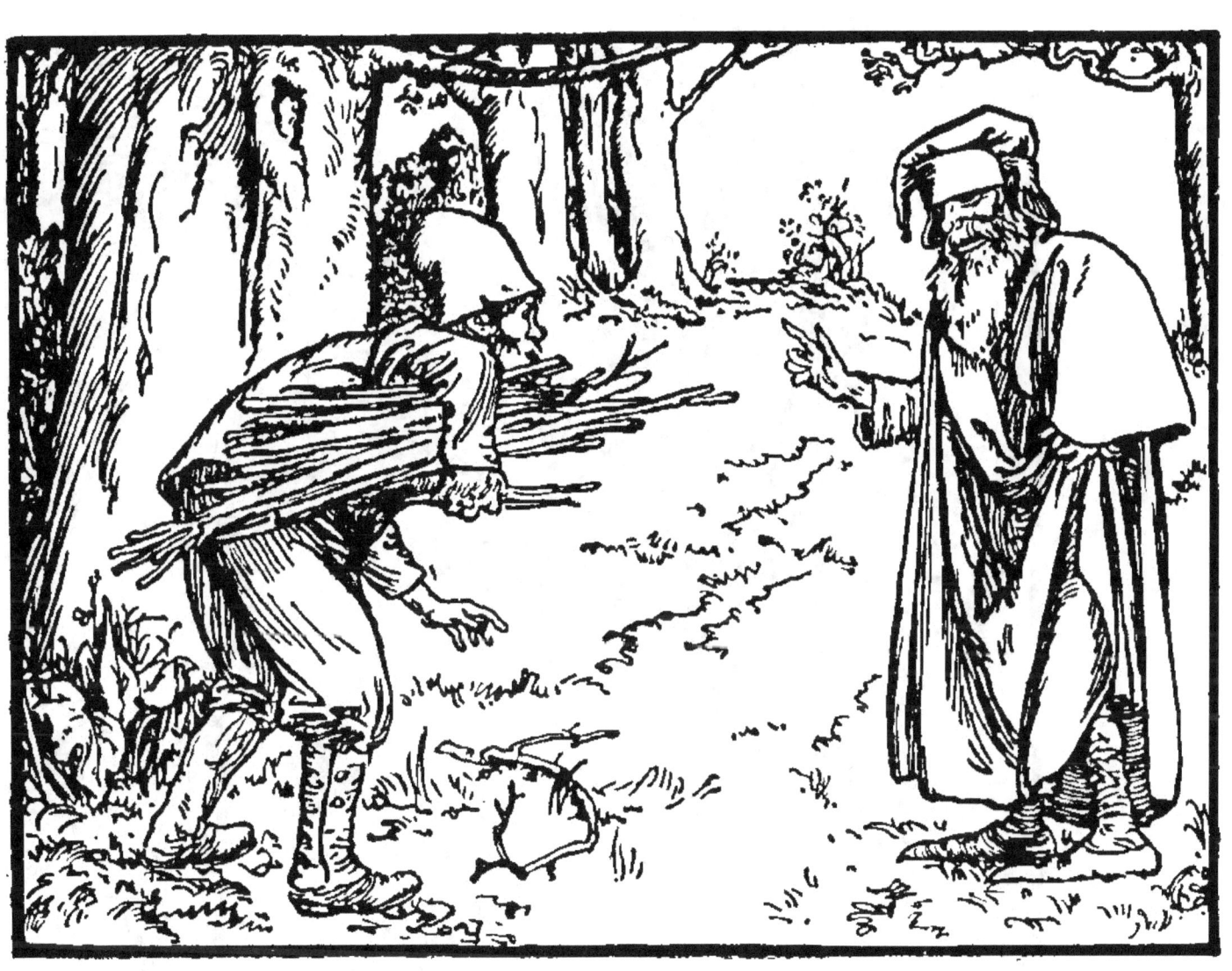

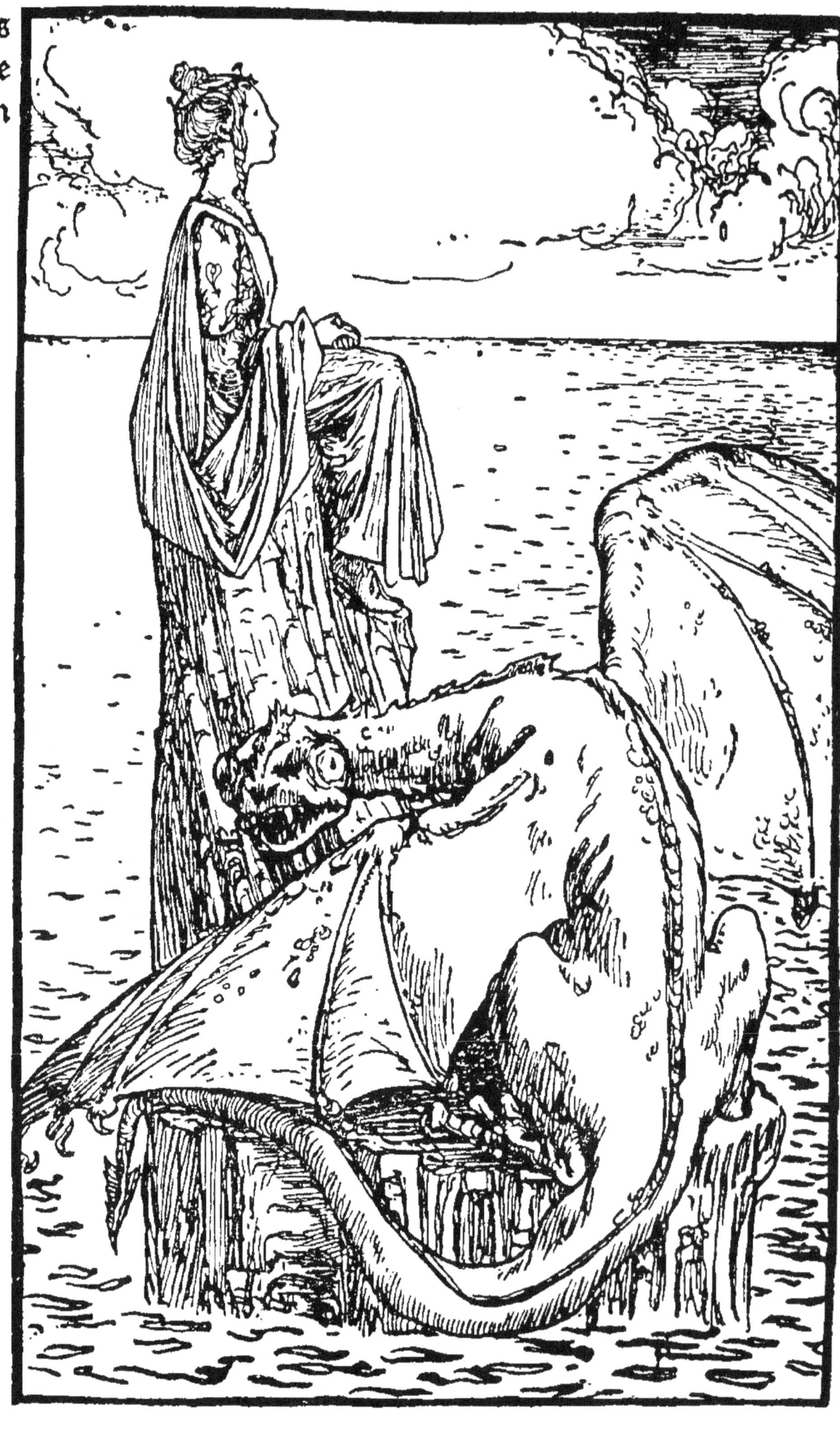

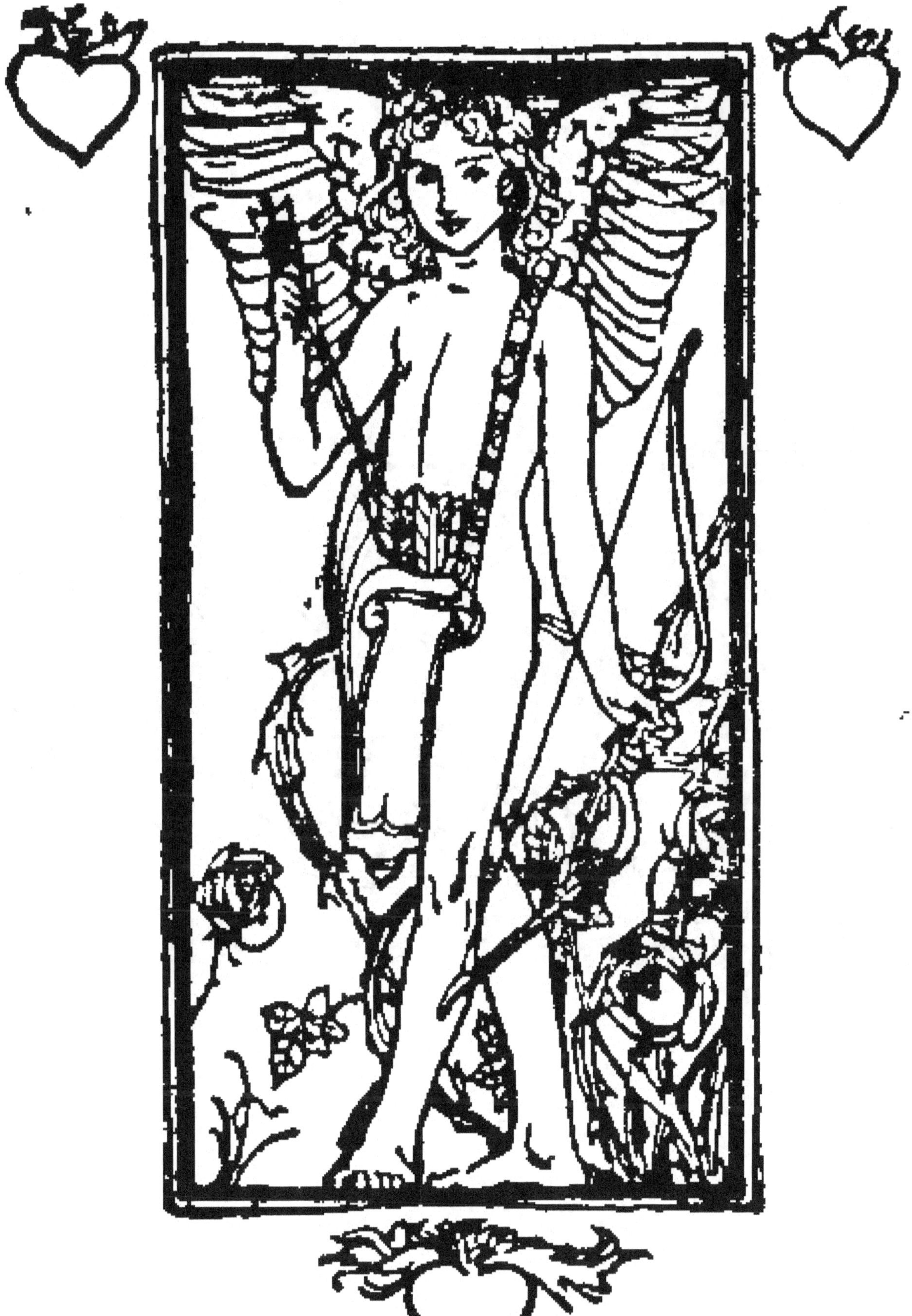

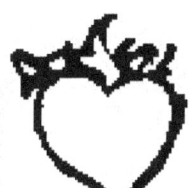

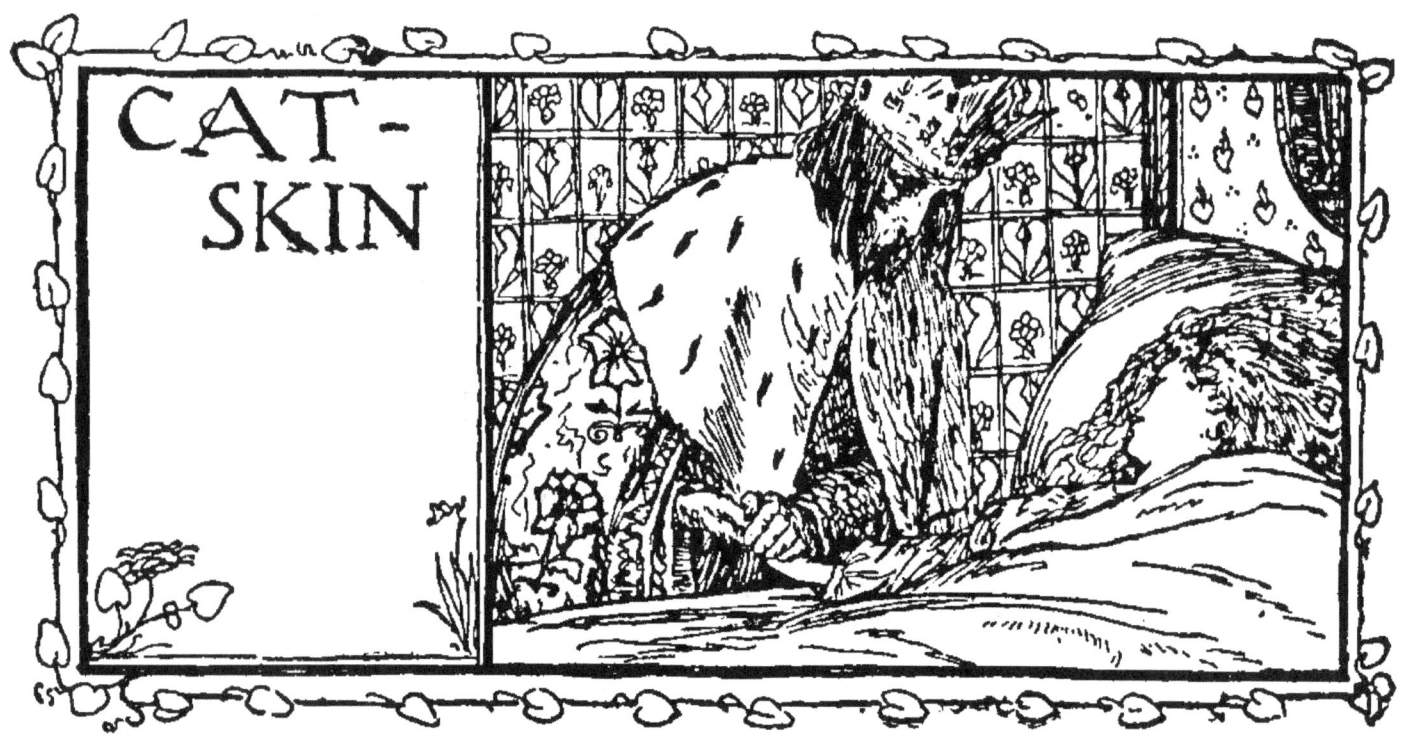

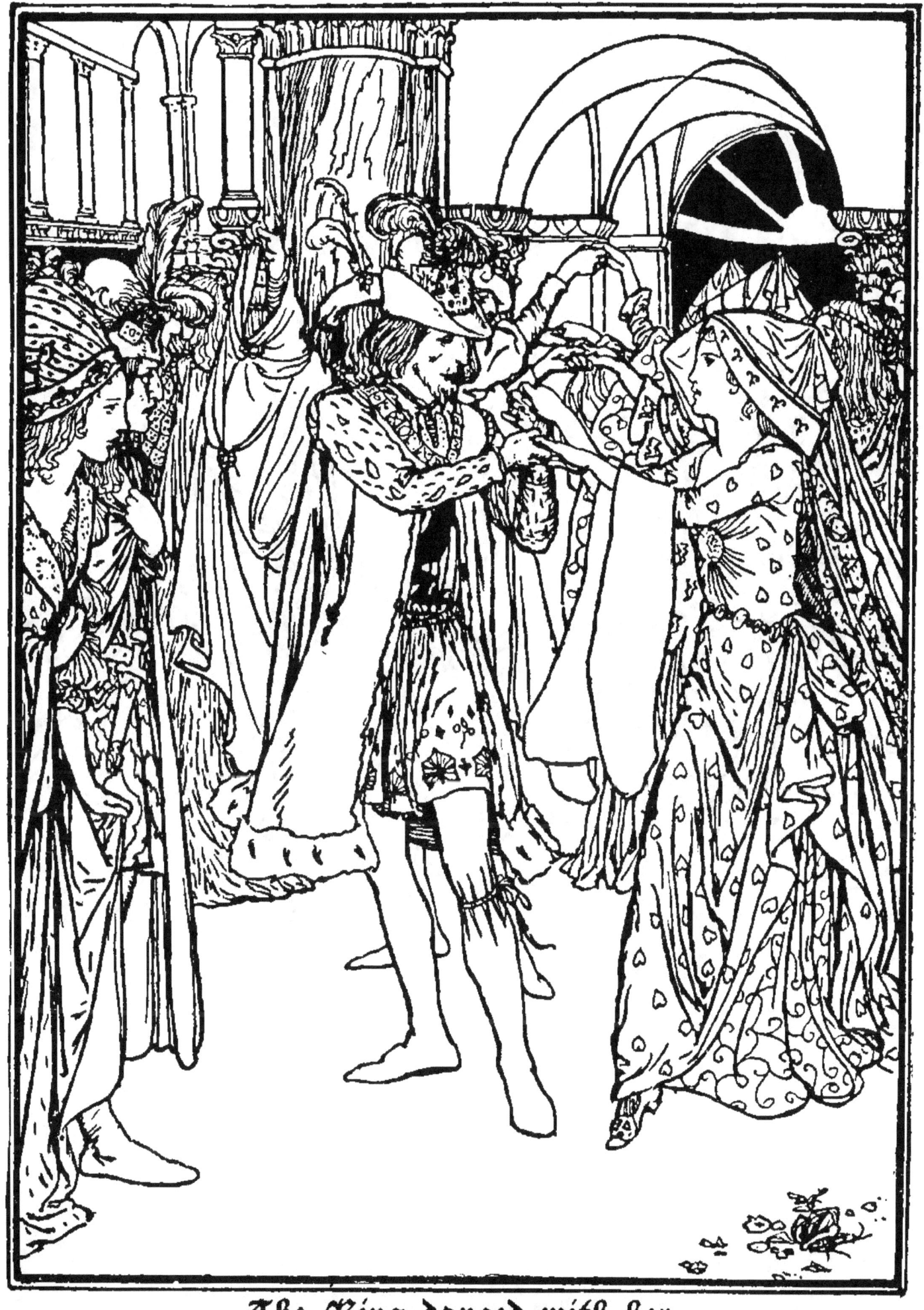

The King danced with her

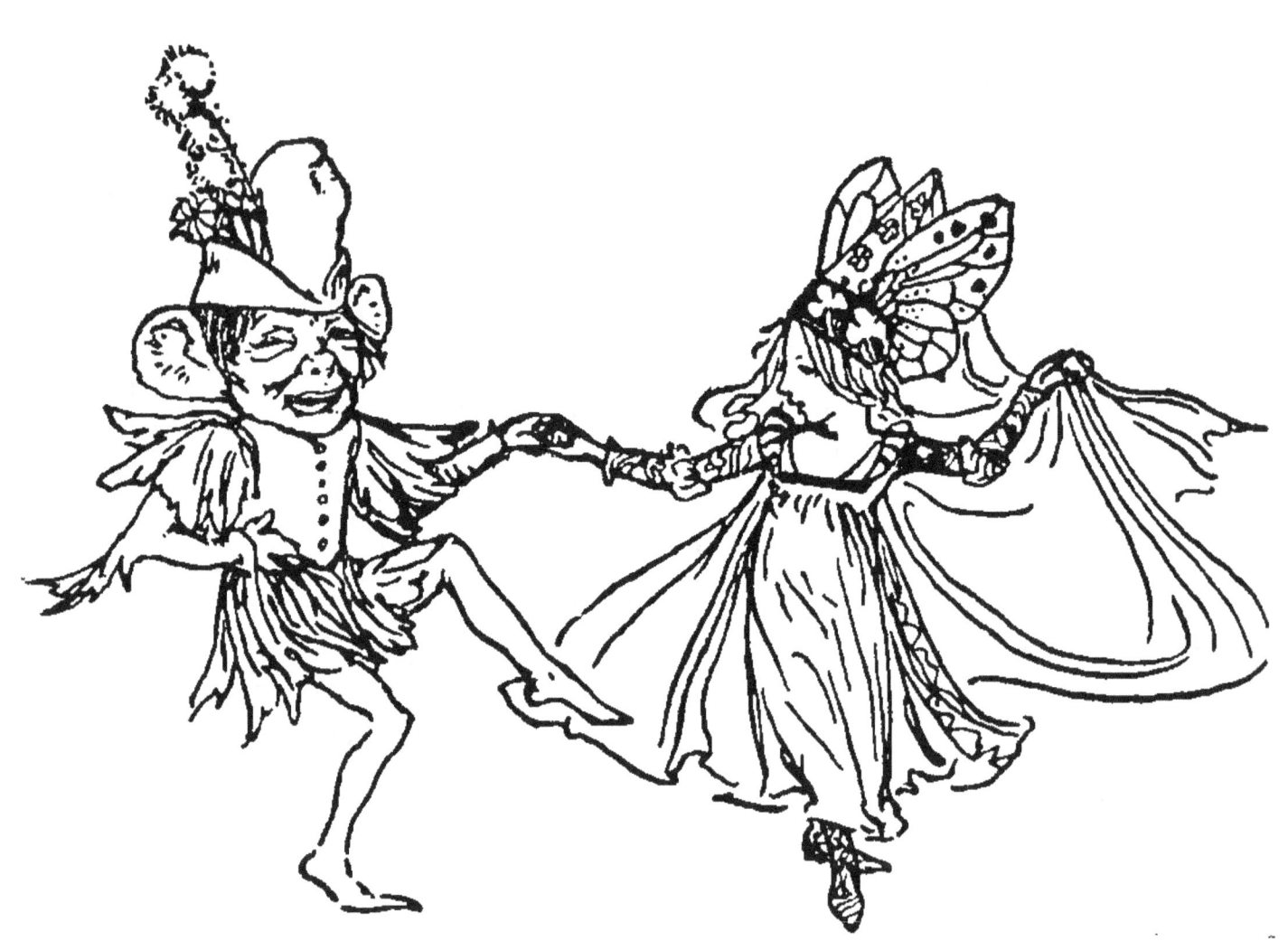

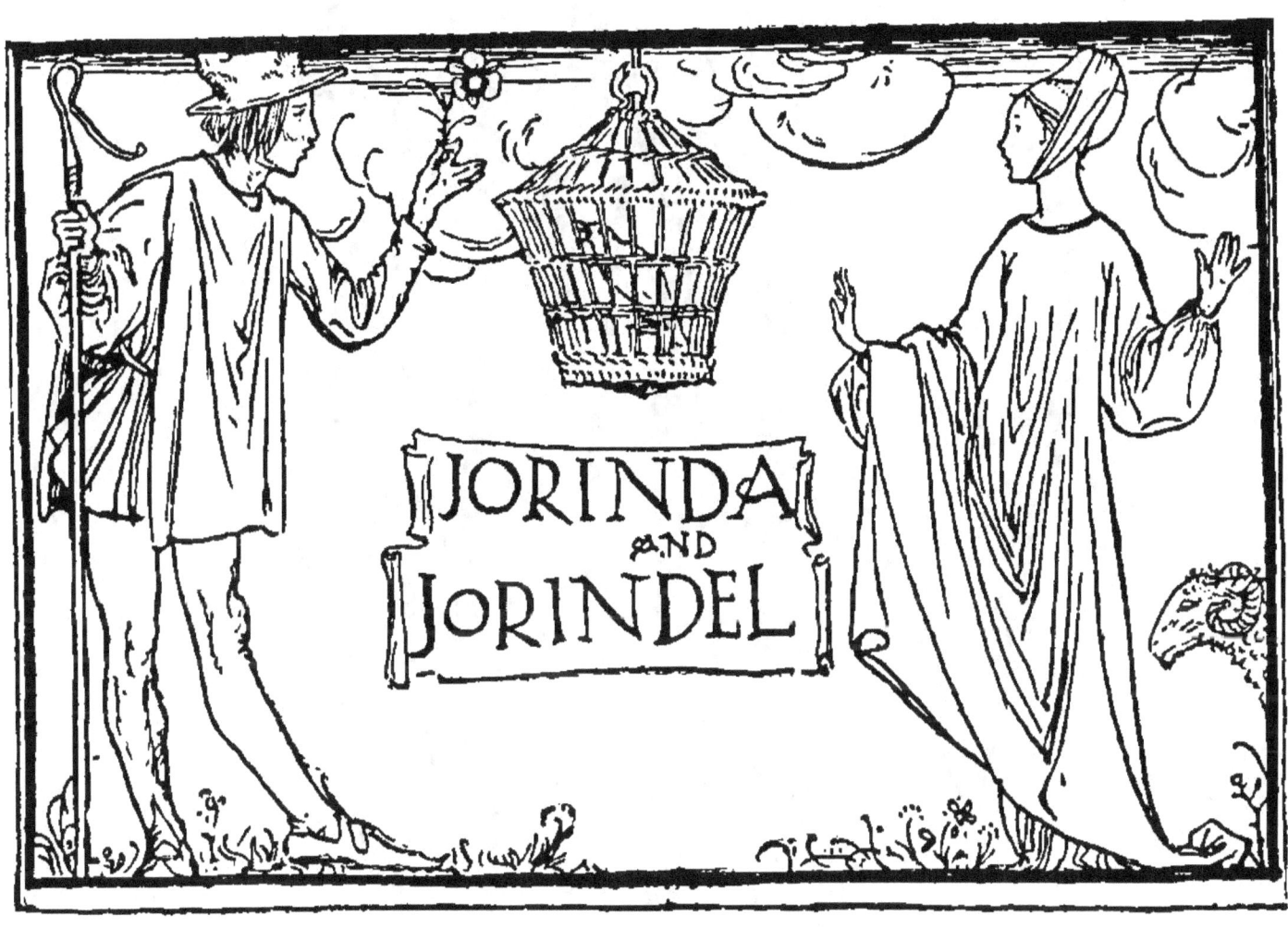

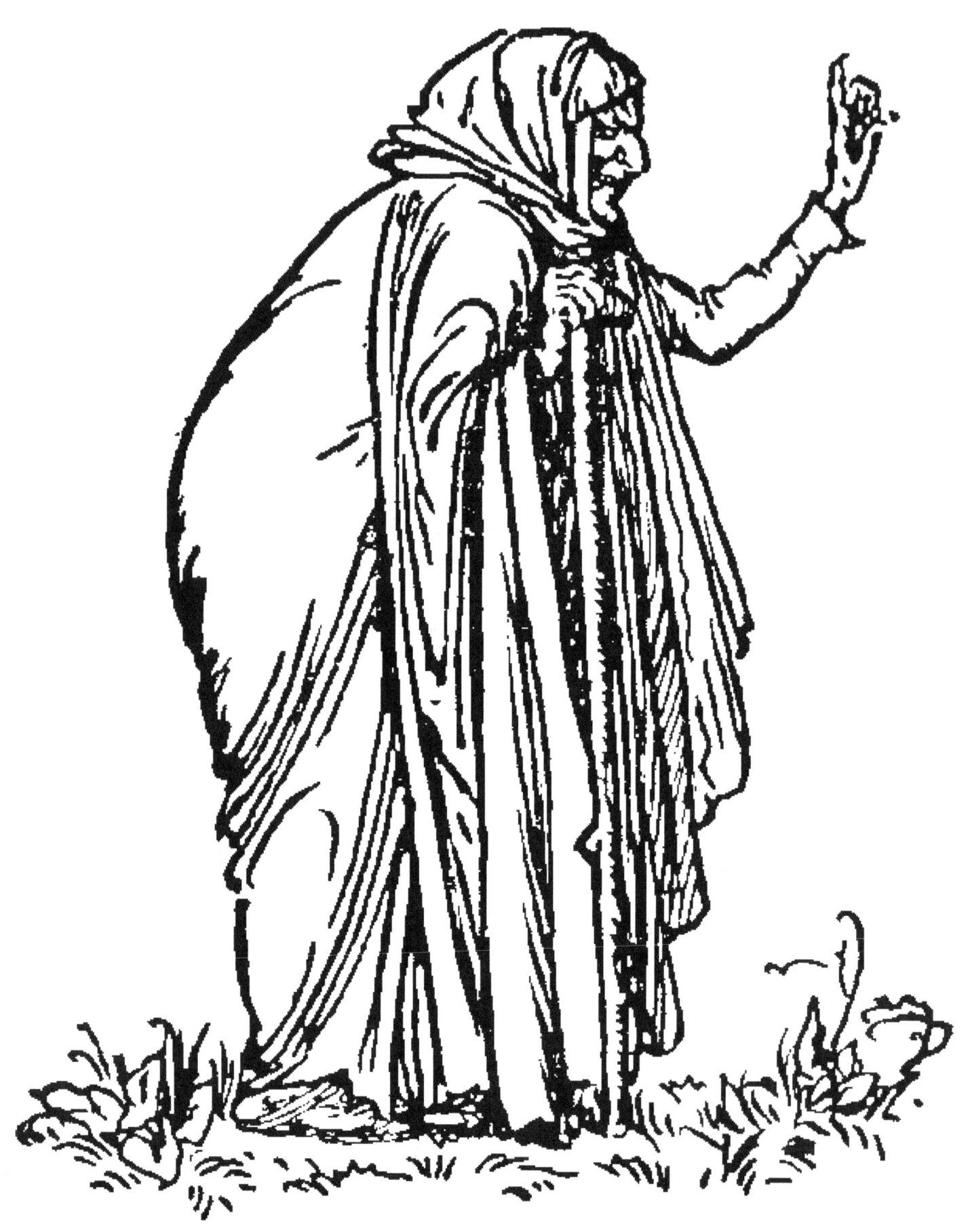

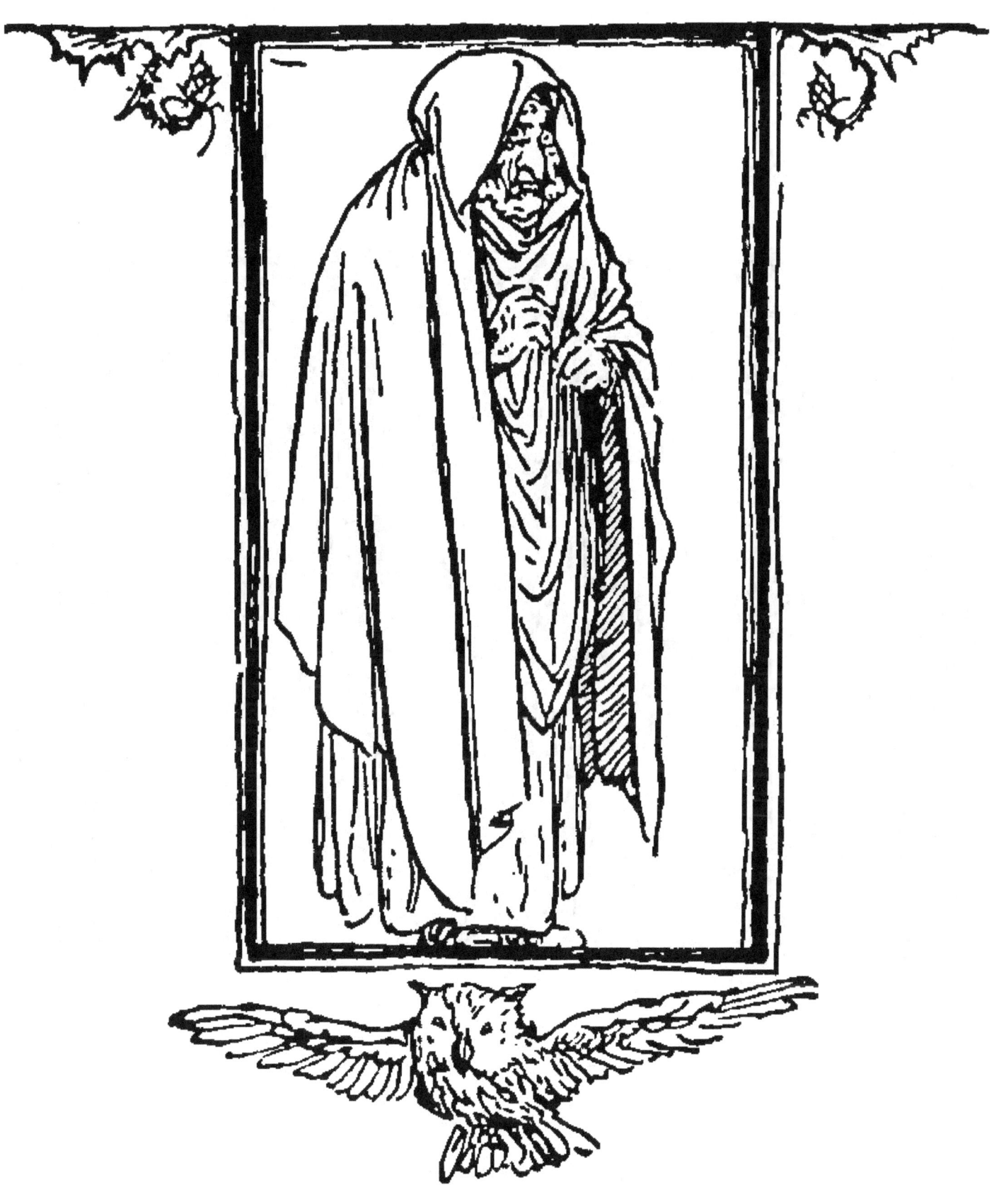

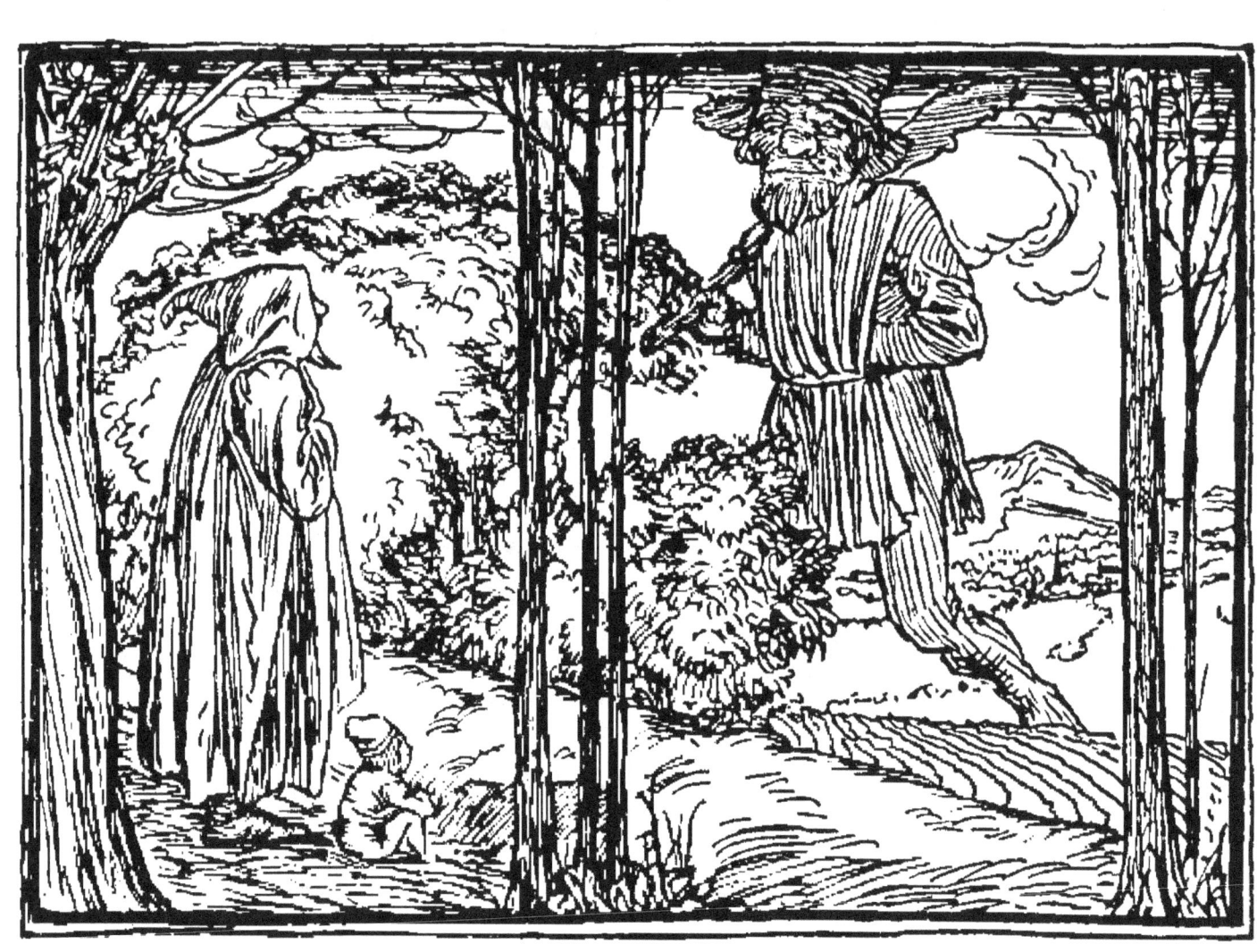

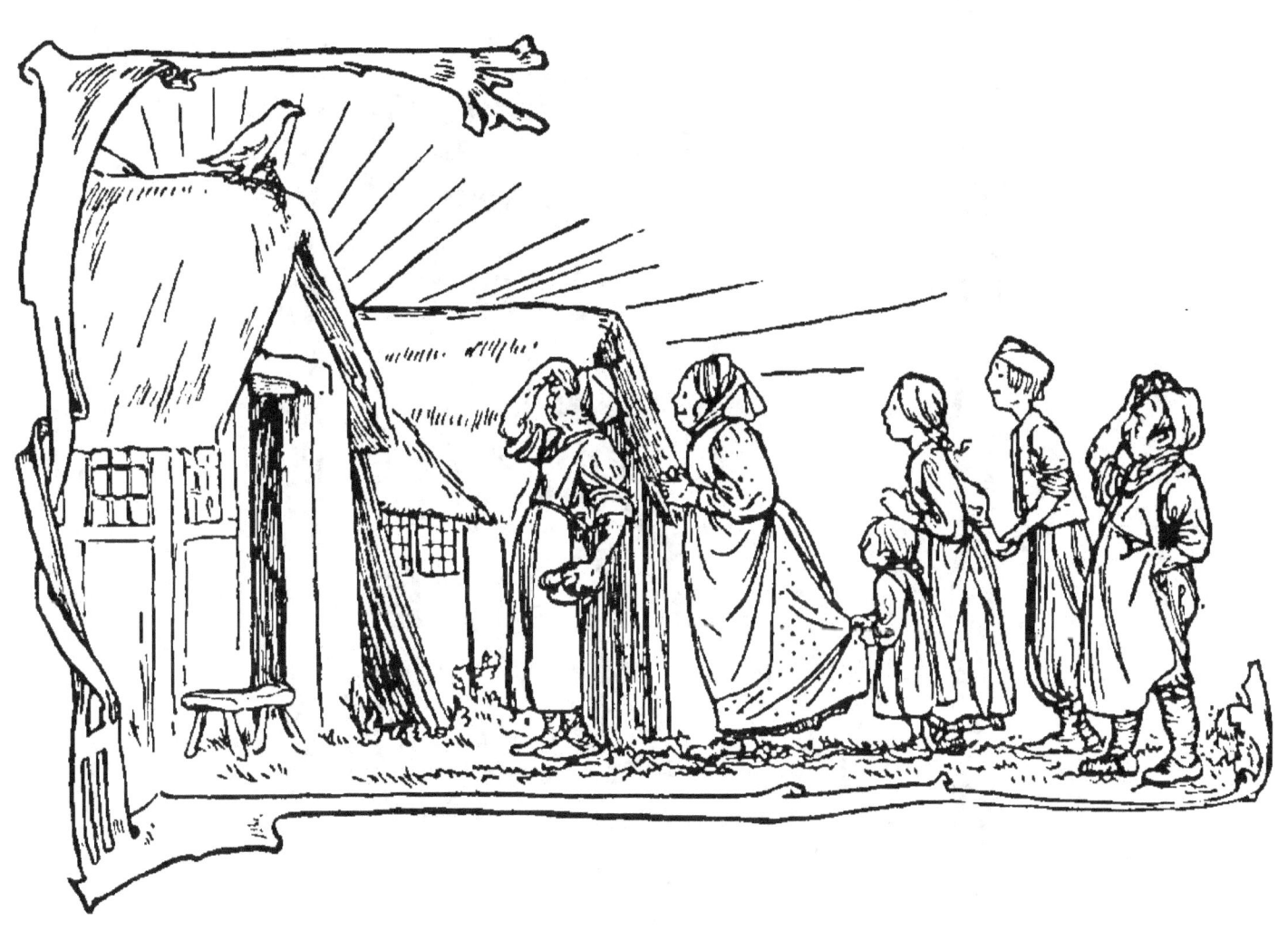

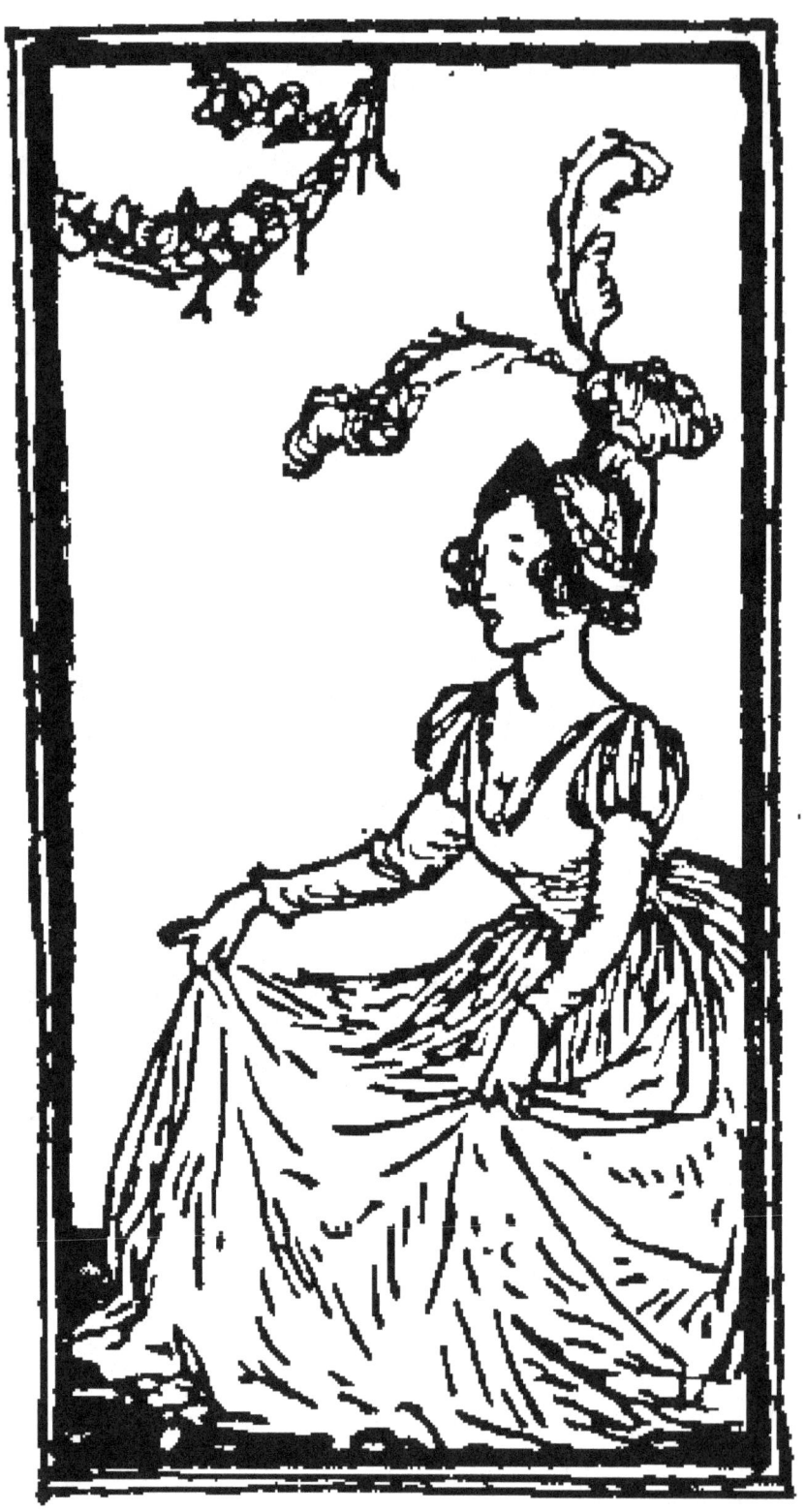

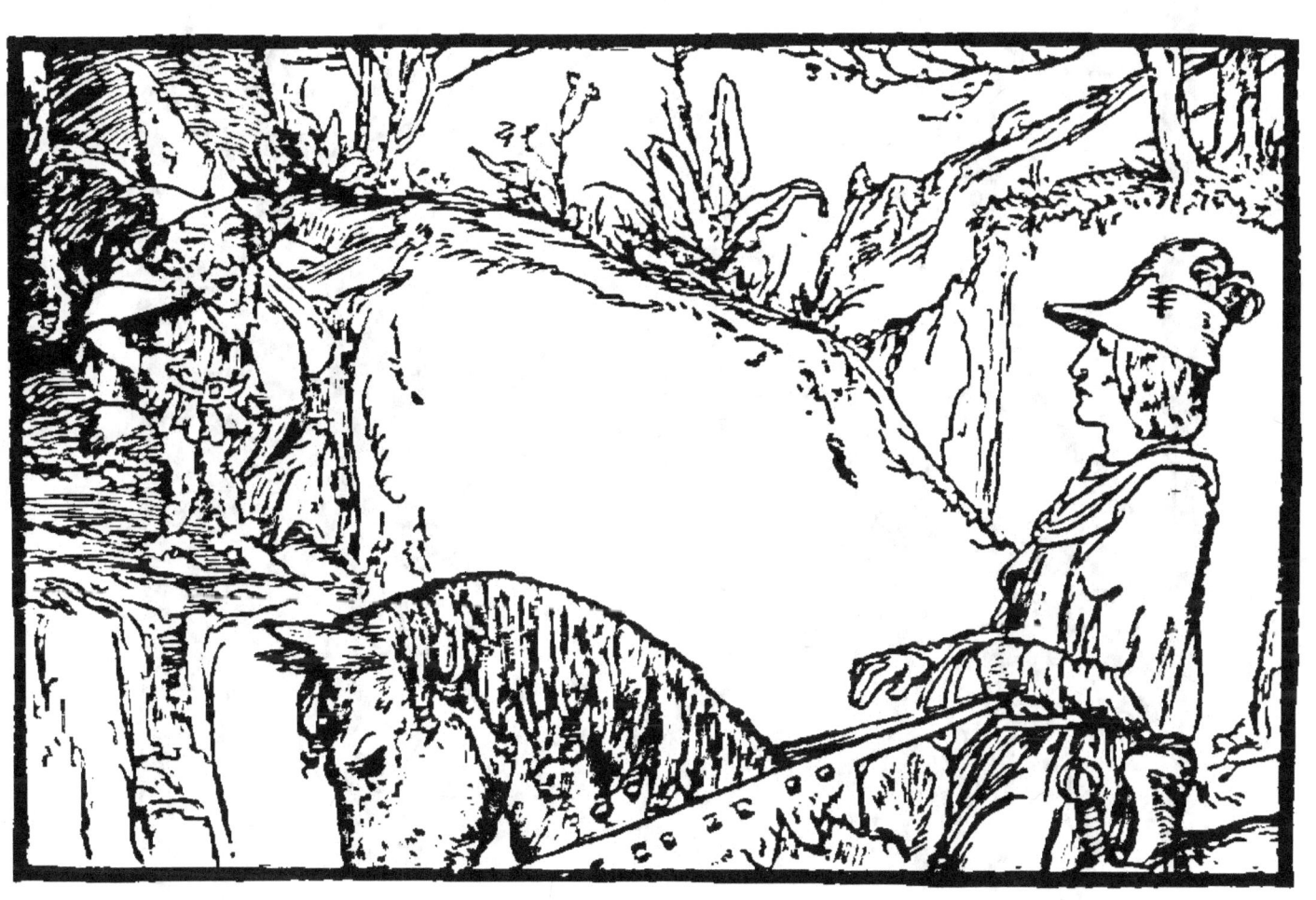

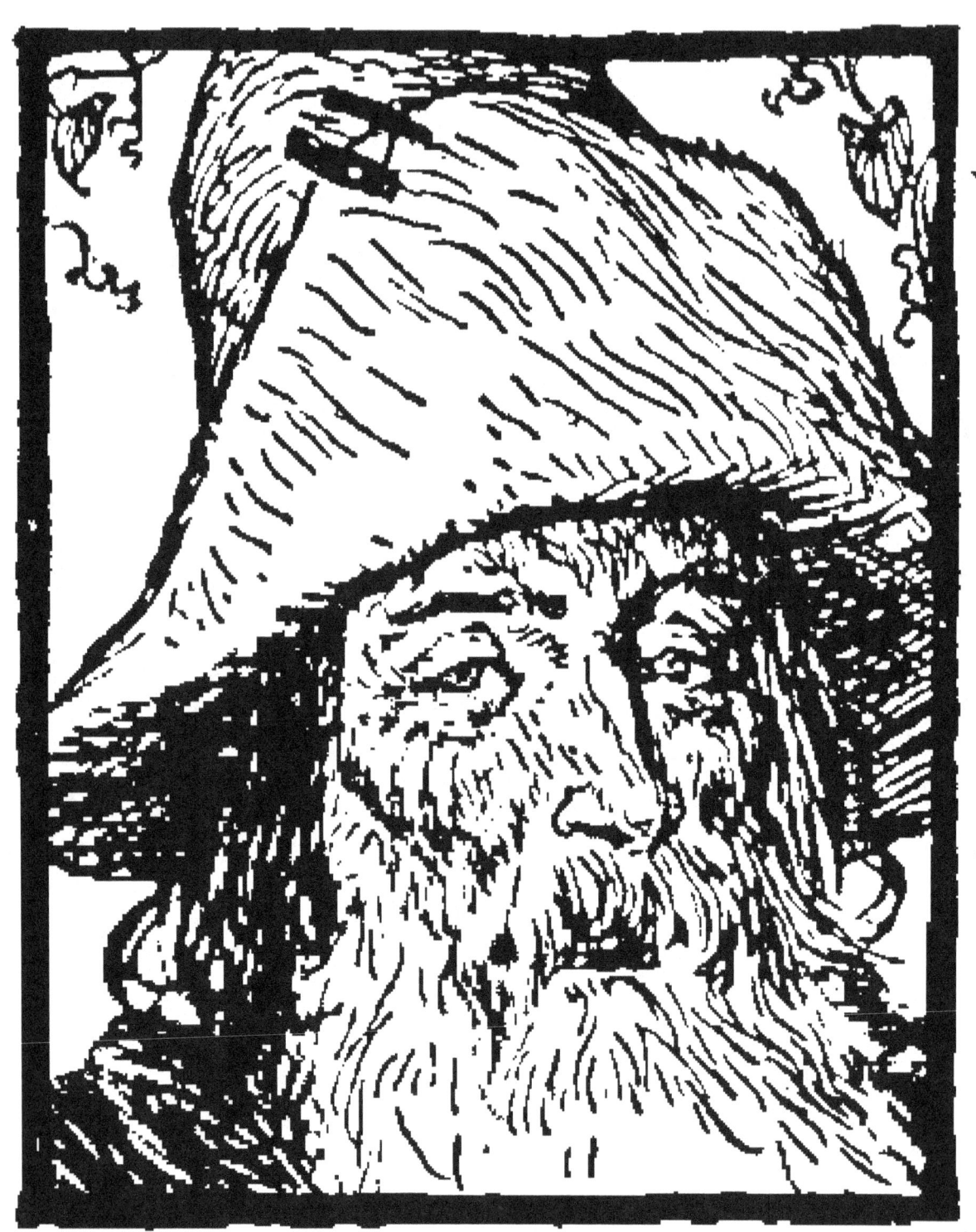

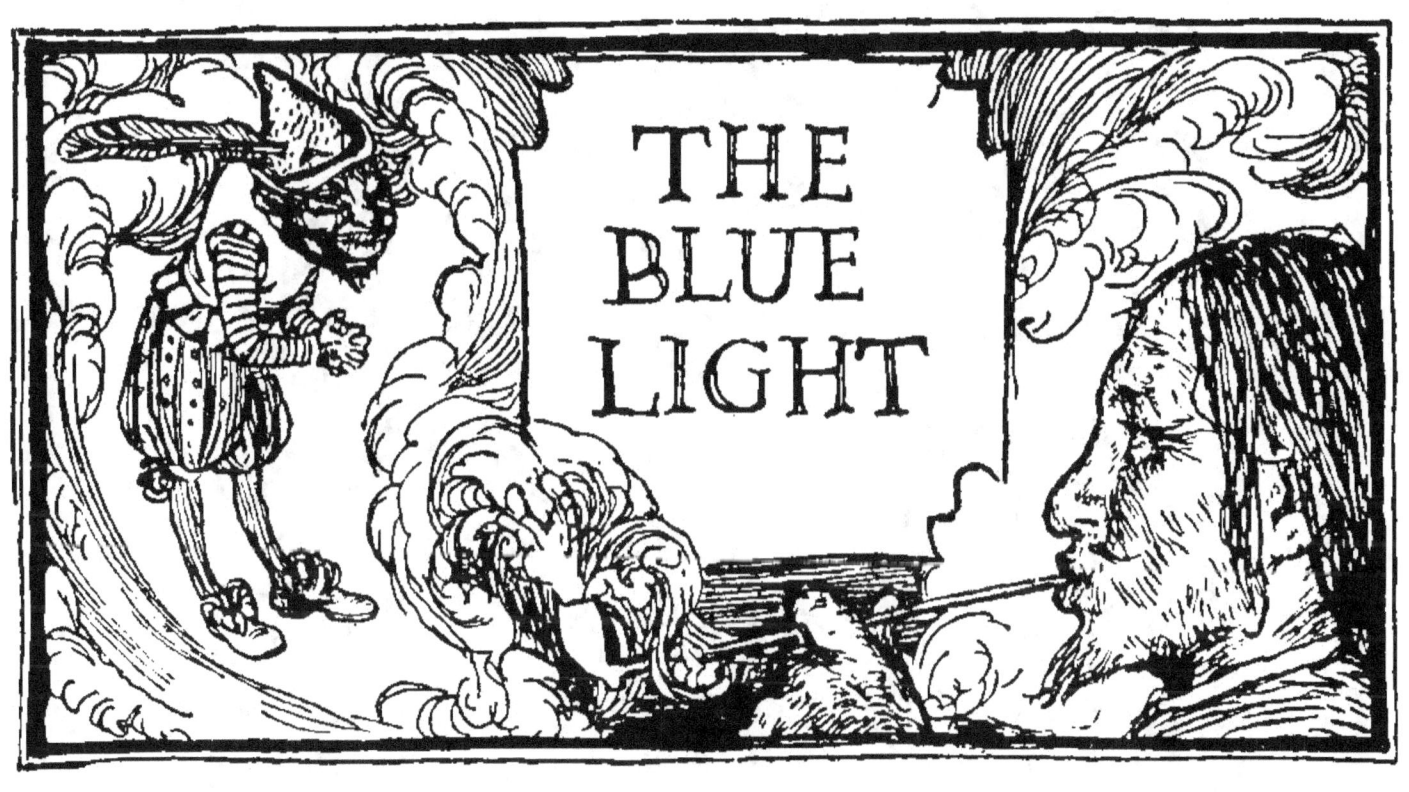

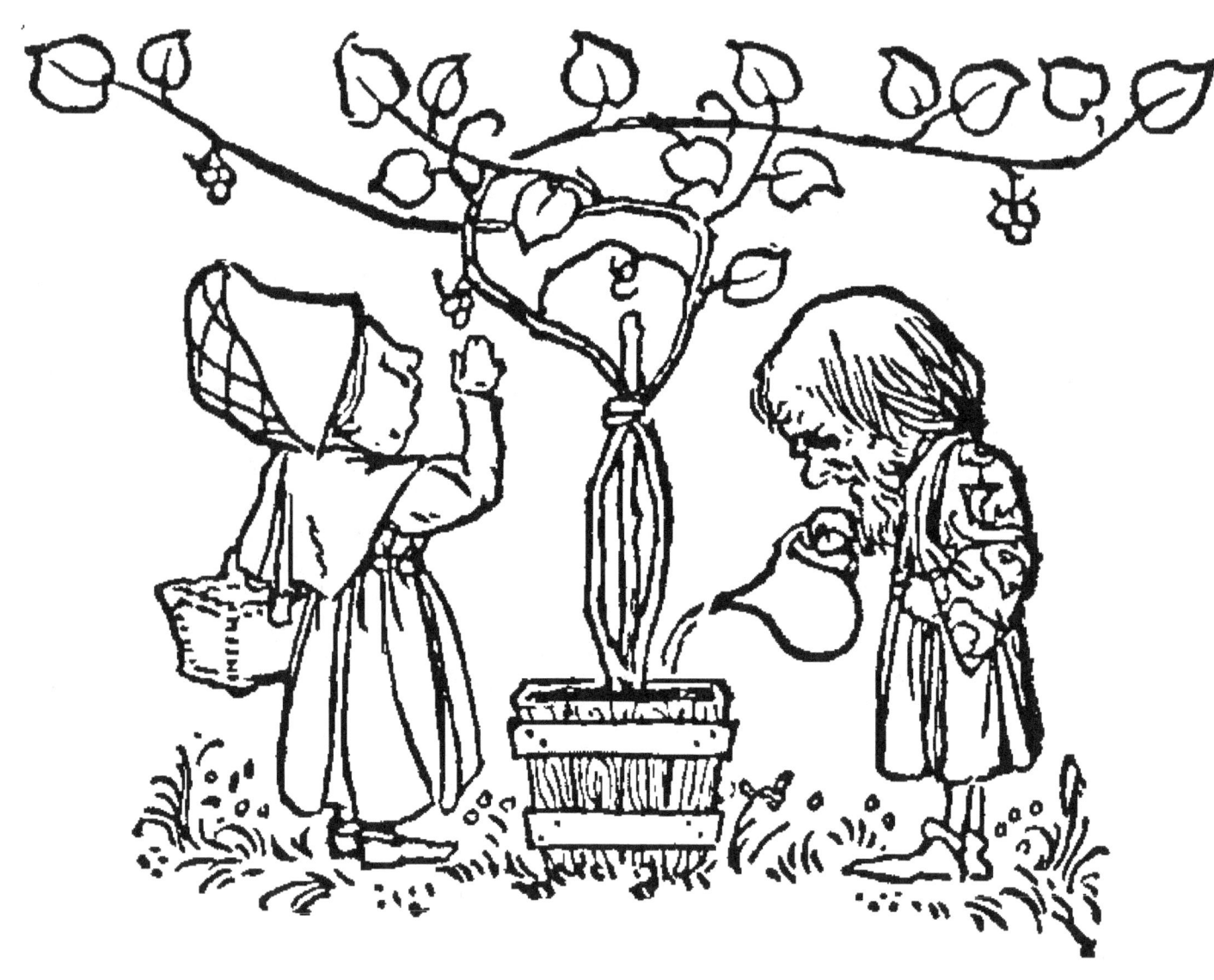

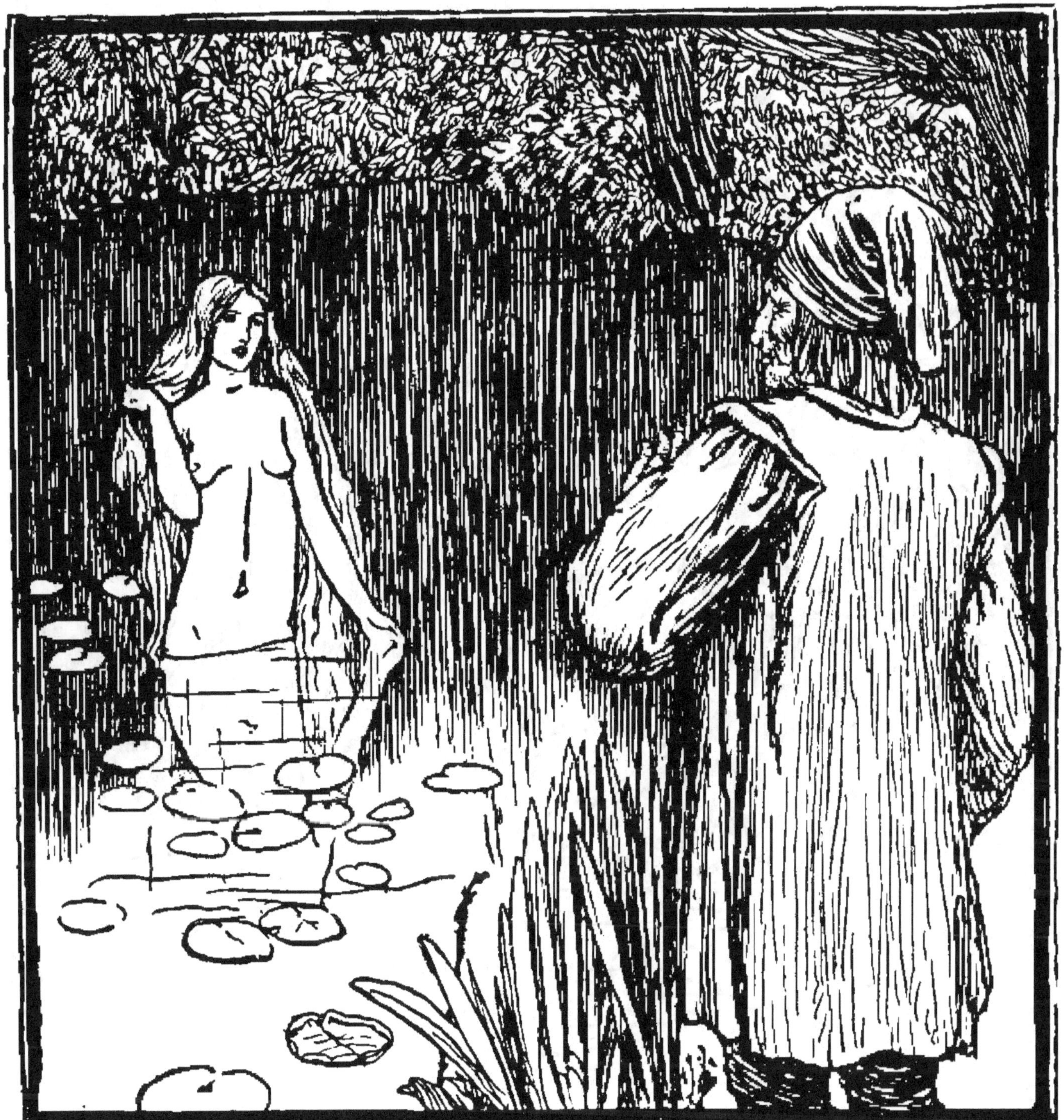

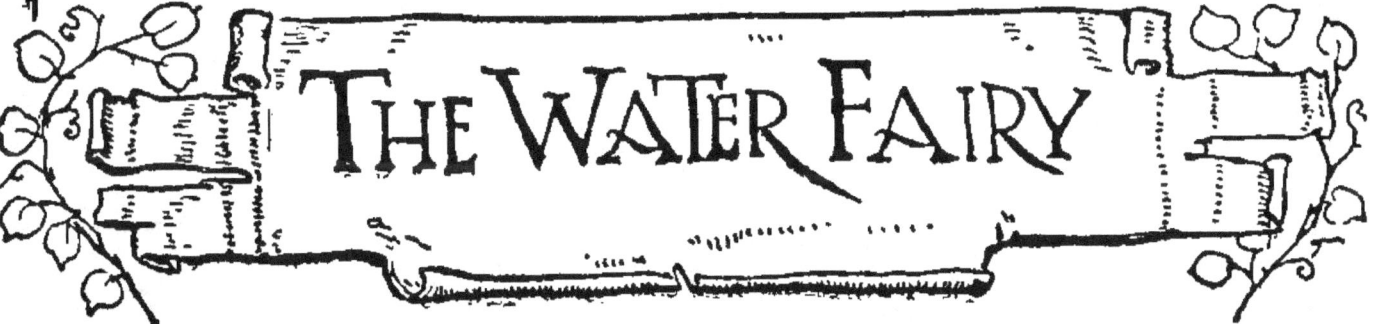

THE WATER FAIRY

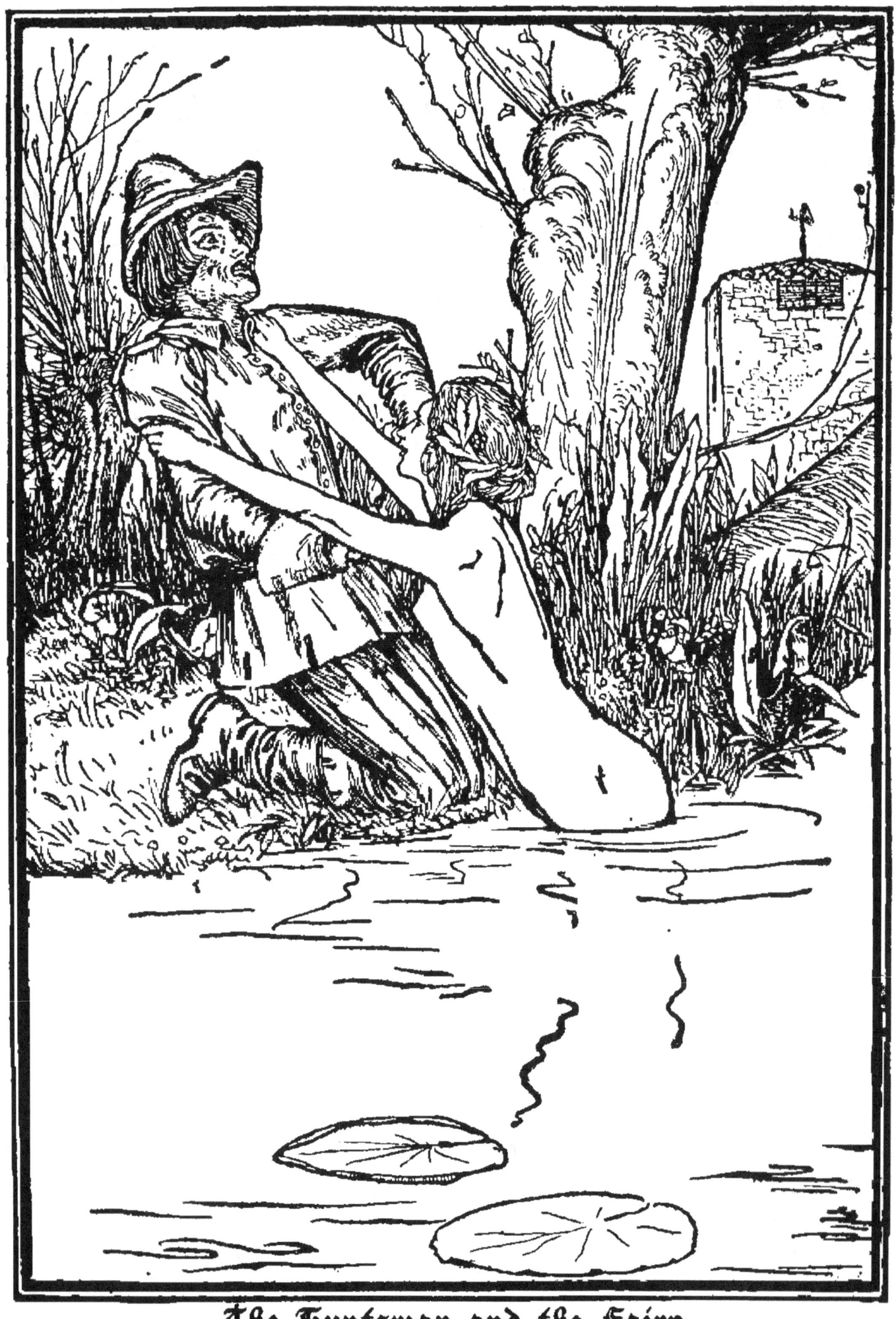

The Huntsman and the Fairy

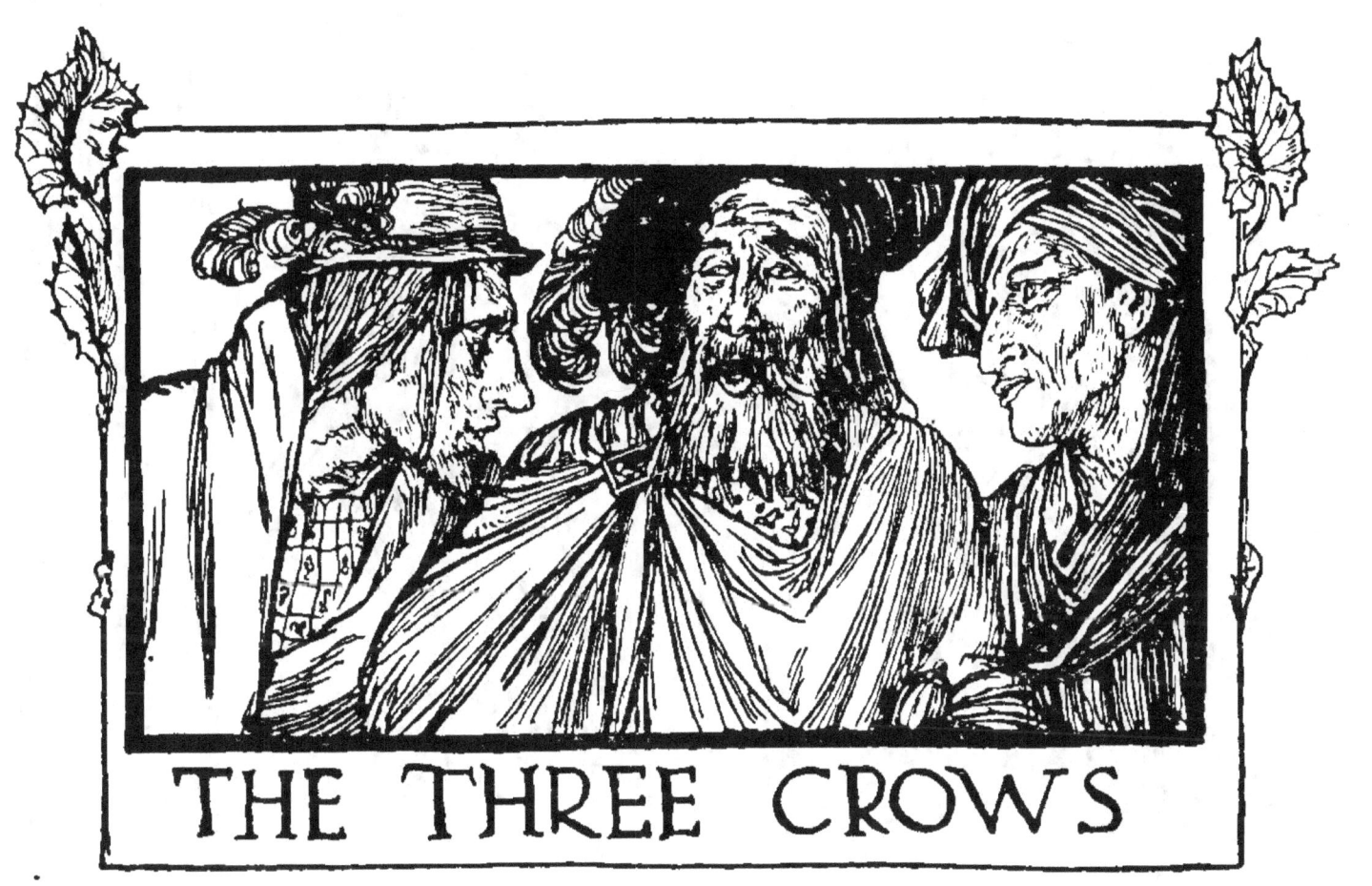

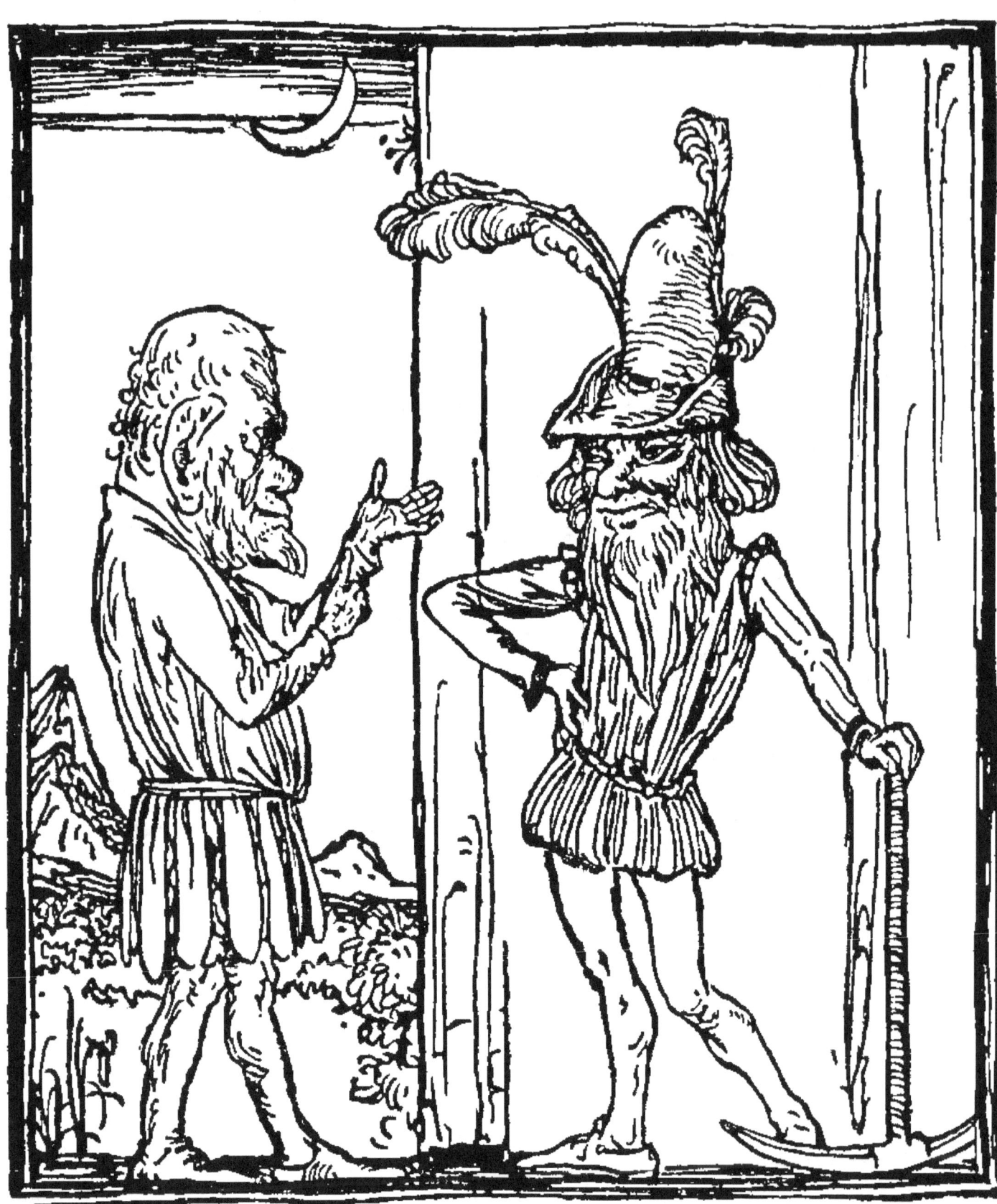

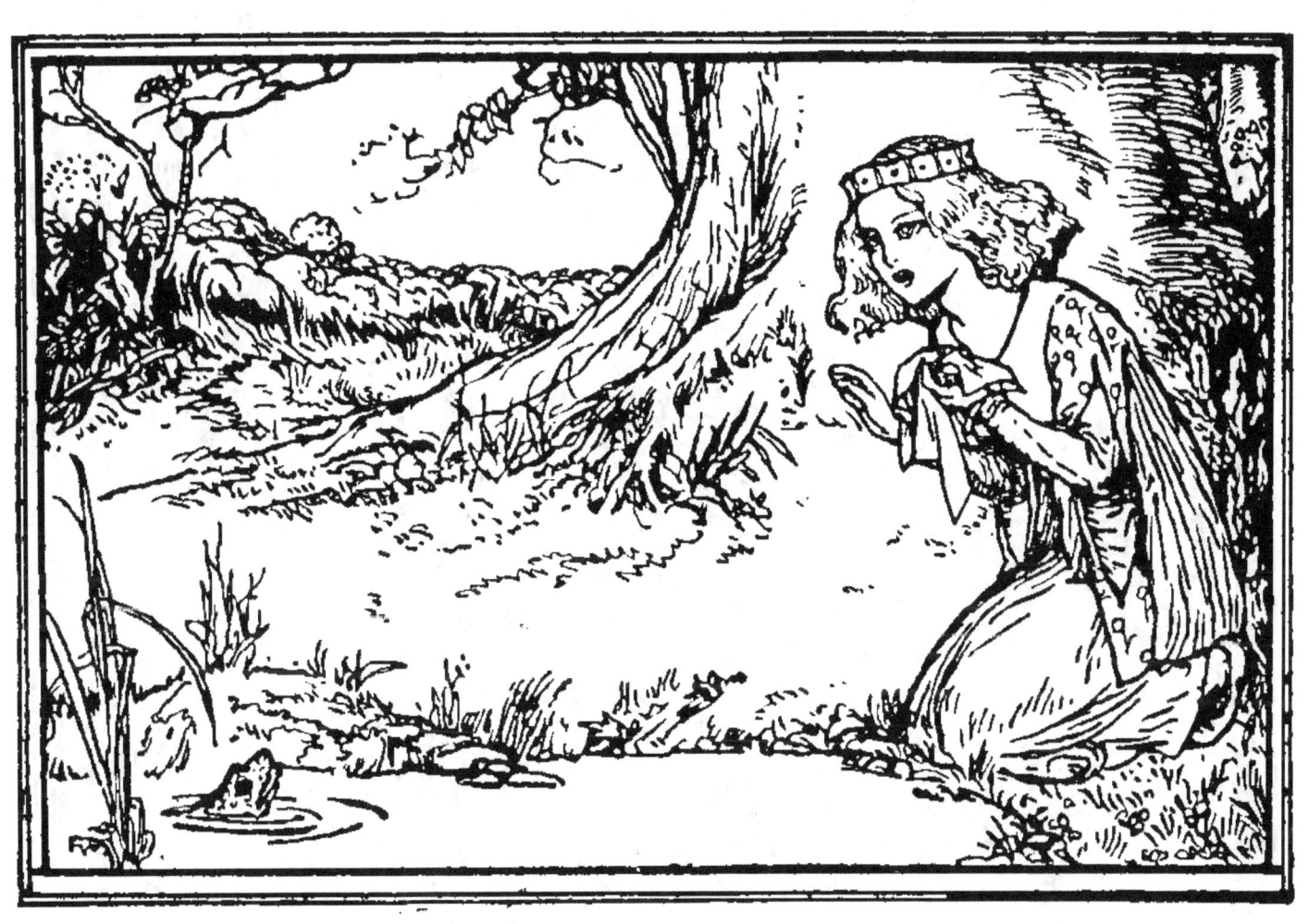

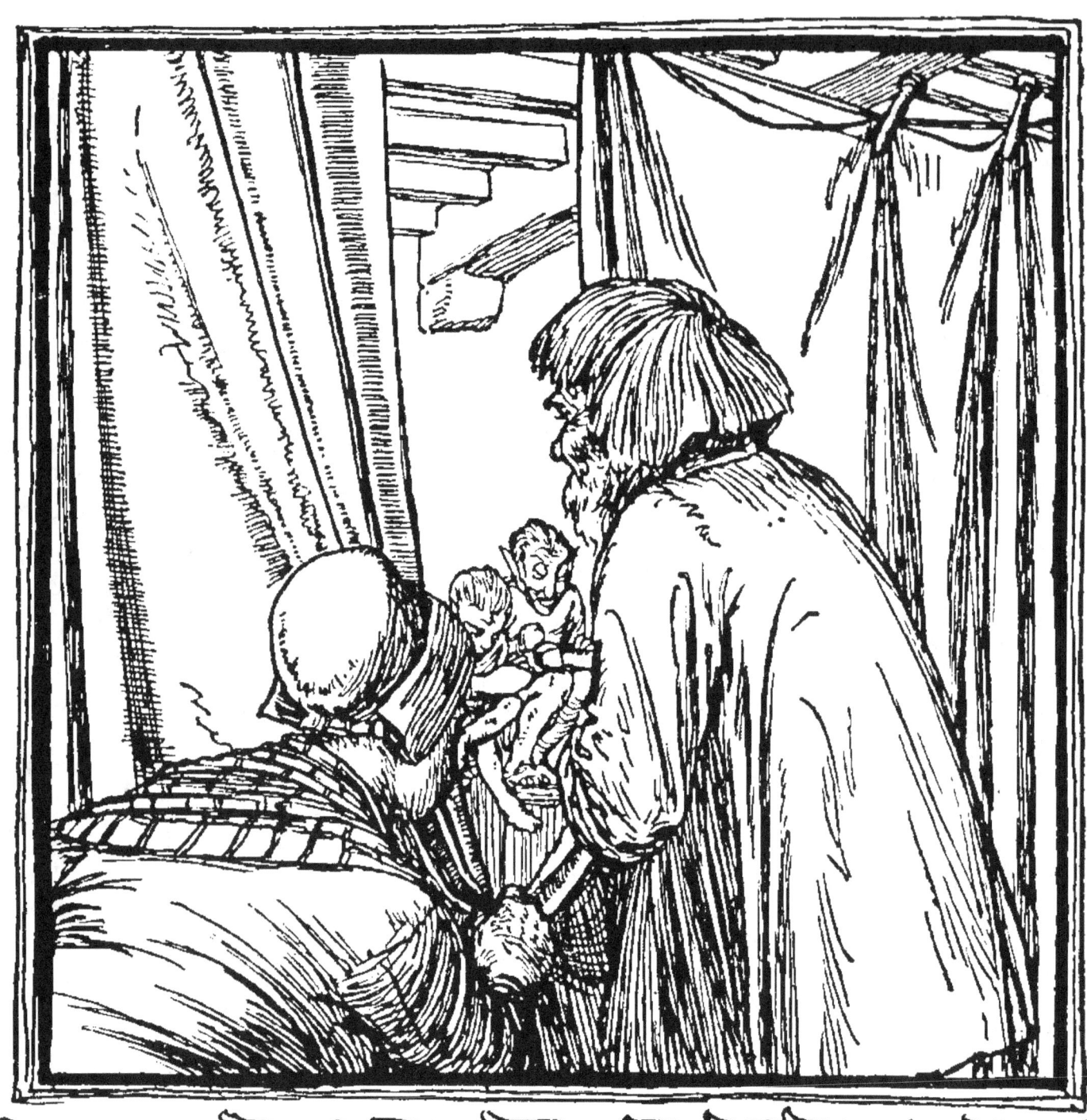

THE ELVES AND THE COBBLER

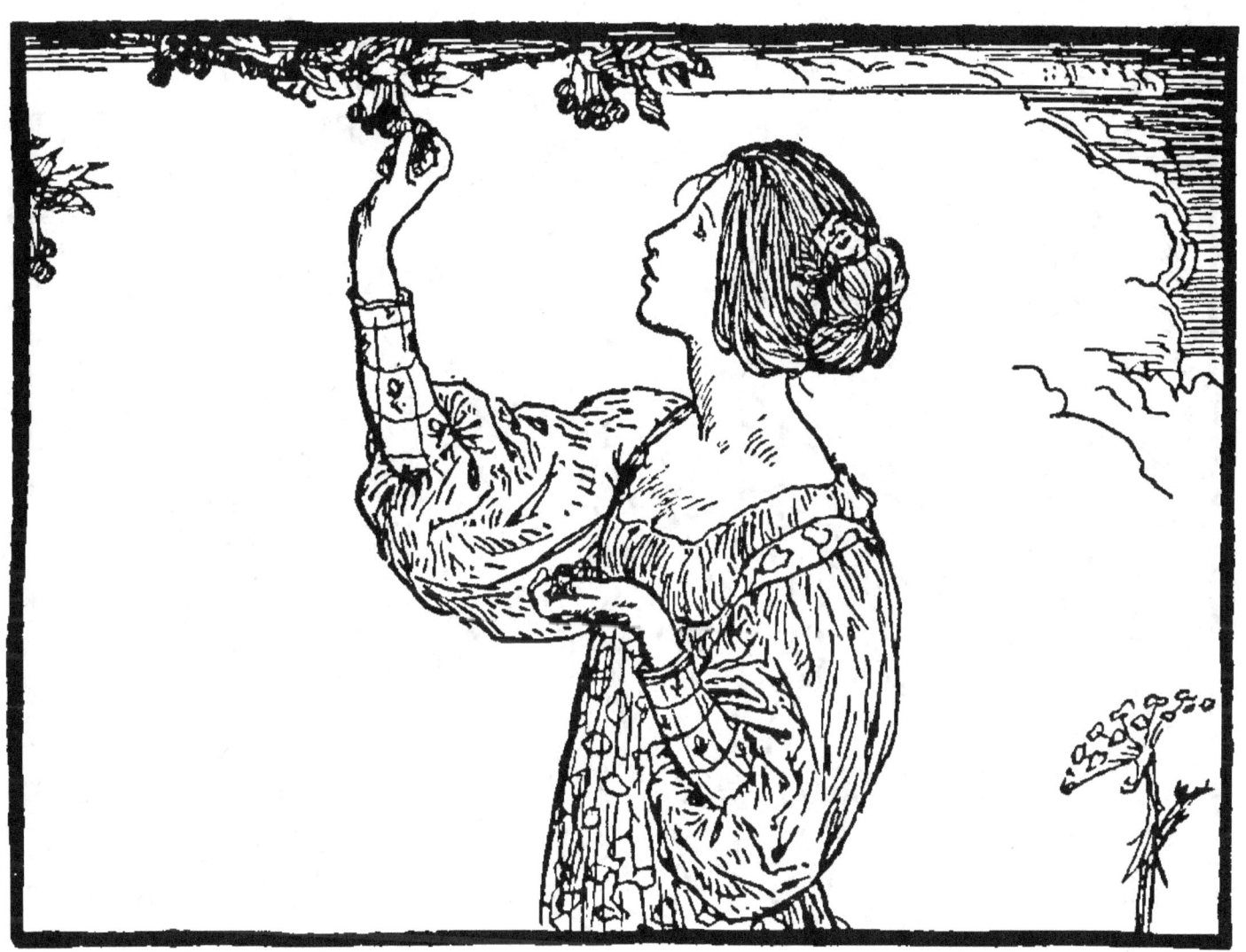

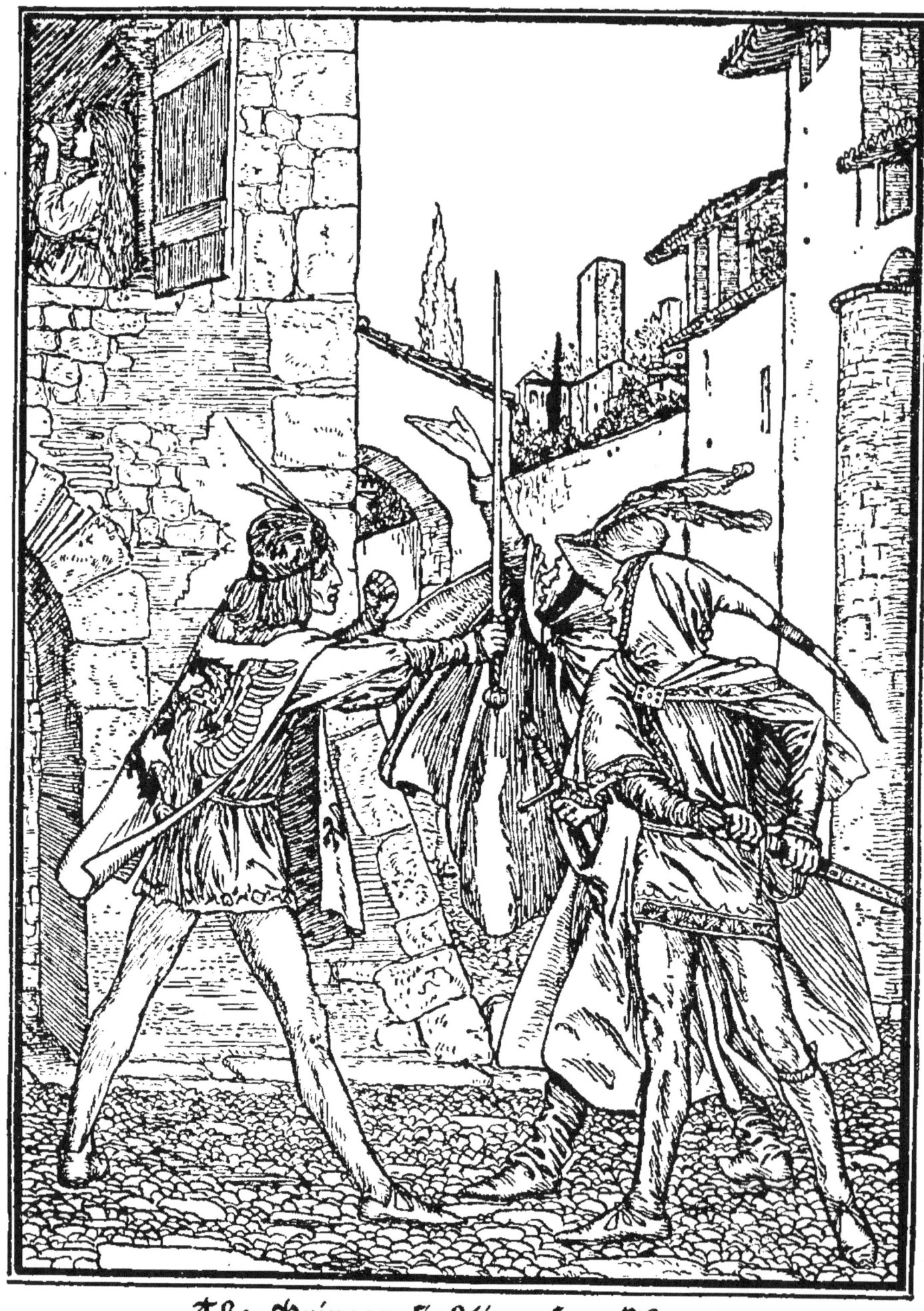

The Princes fighting for Cherry

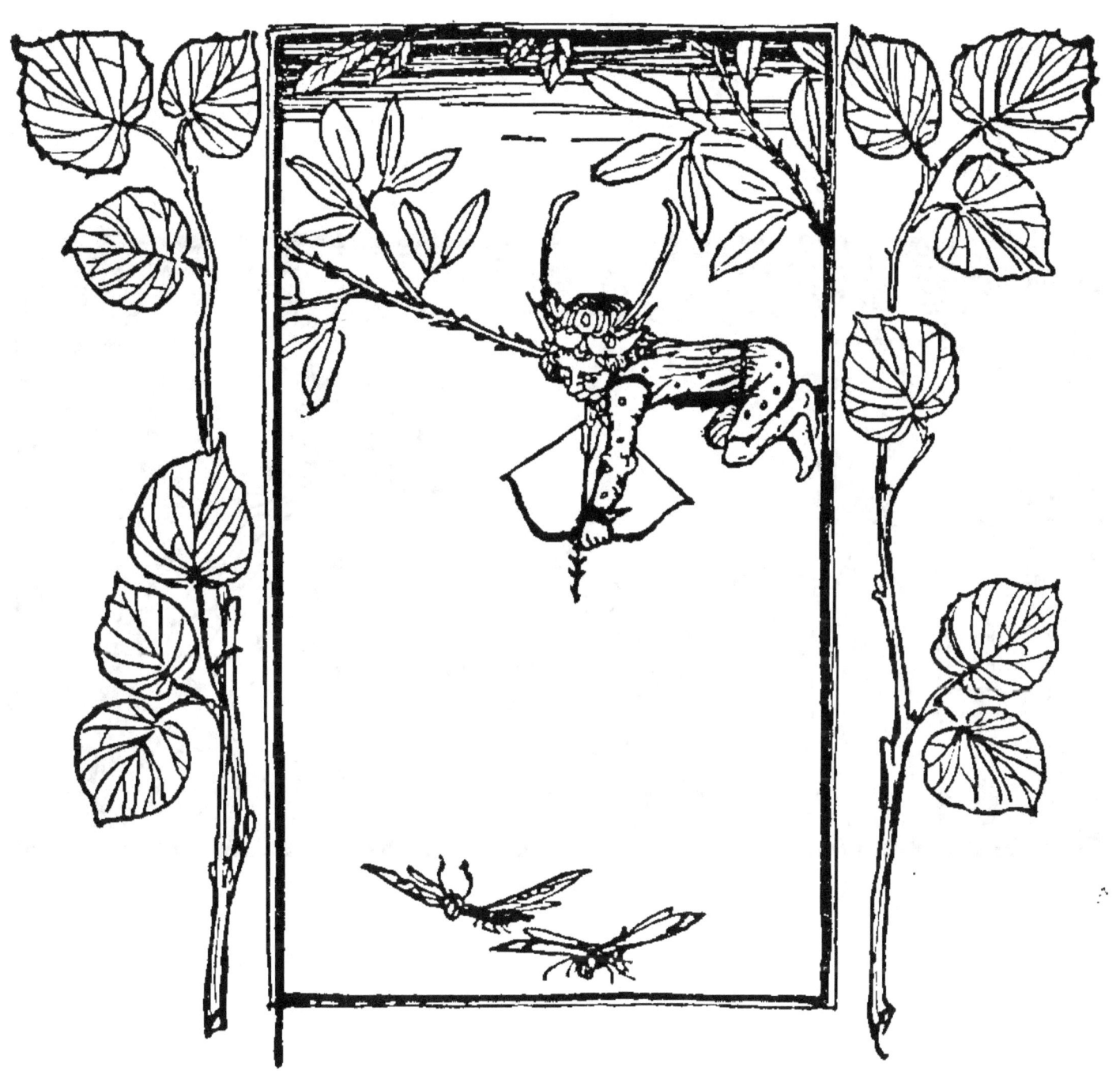

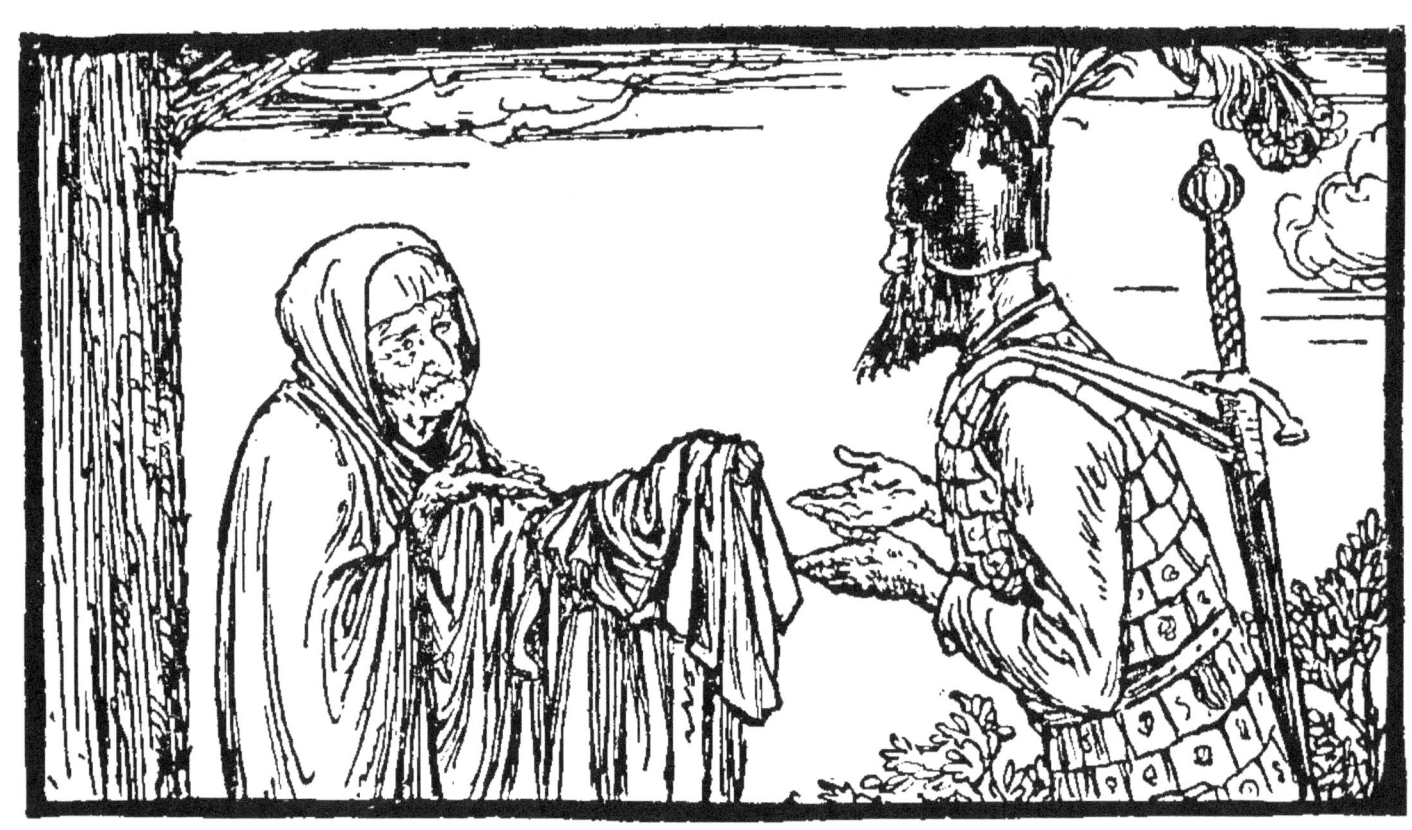

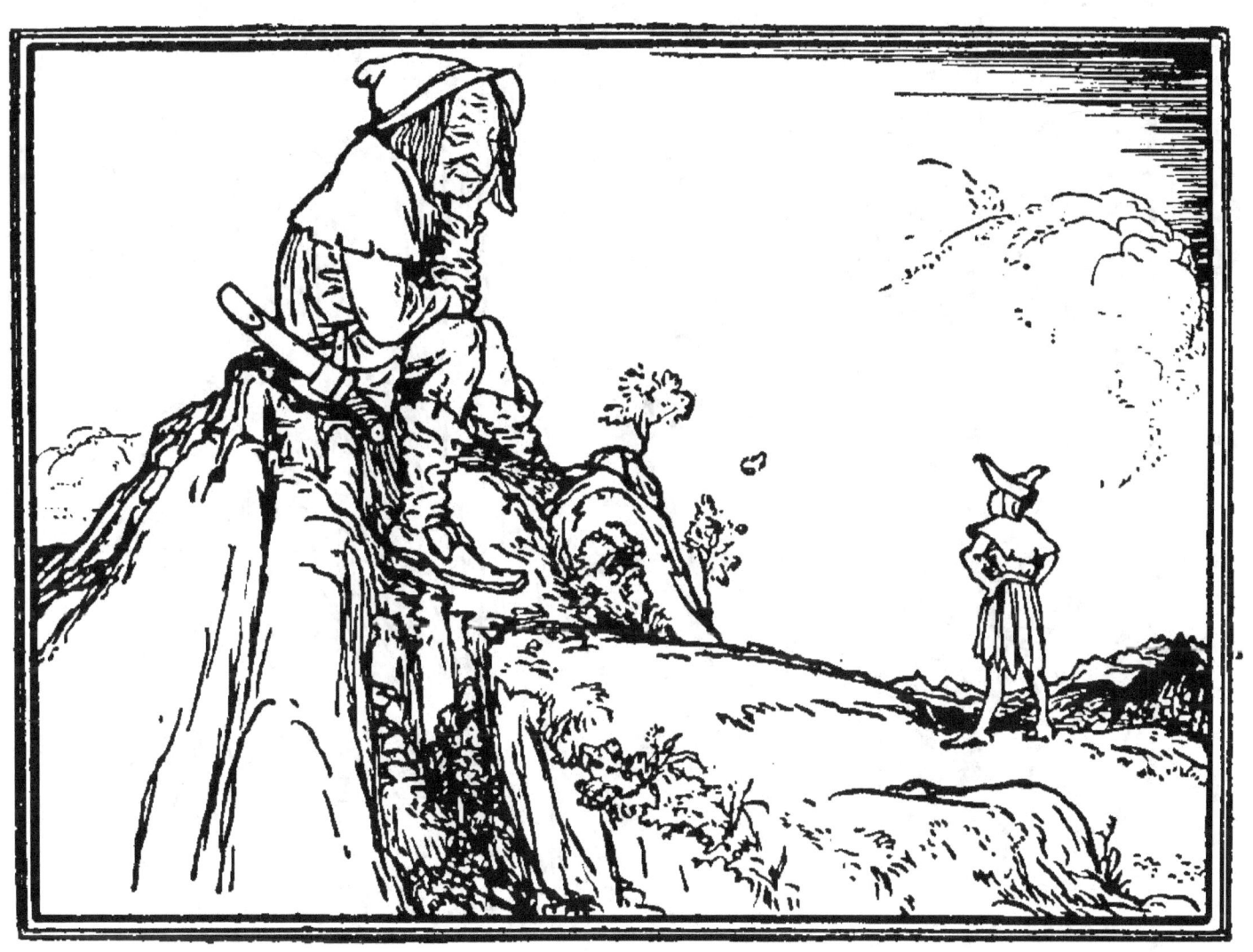

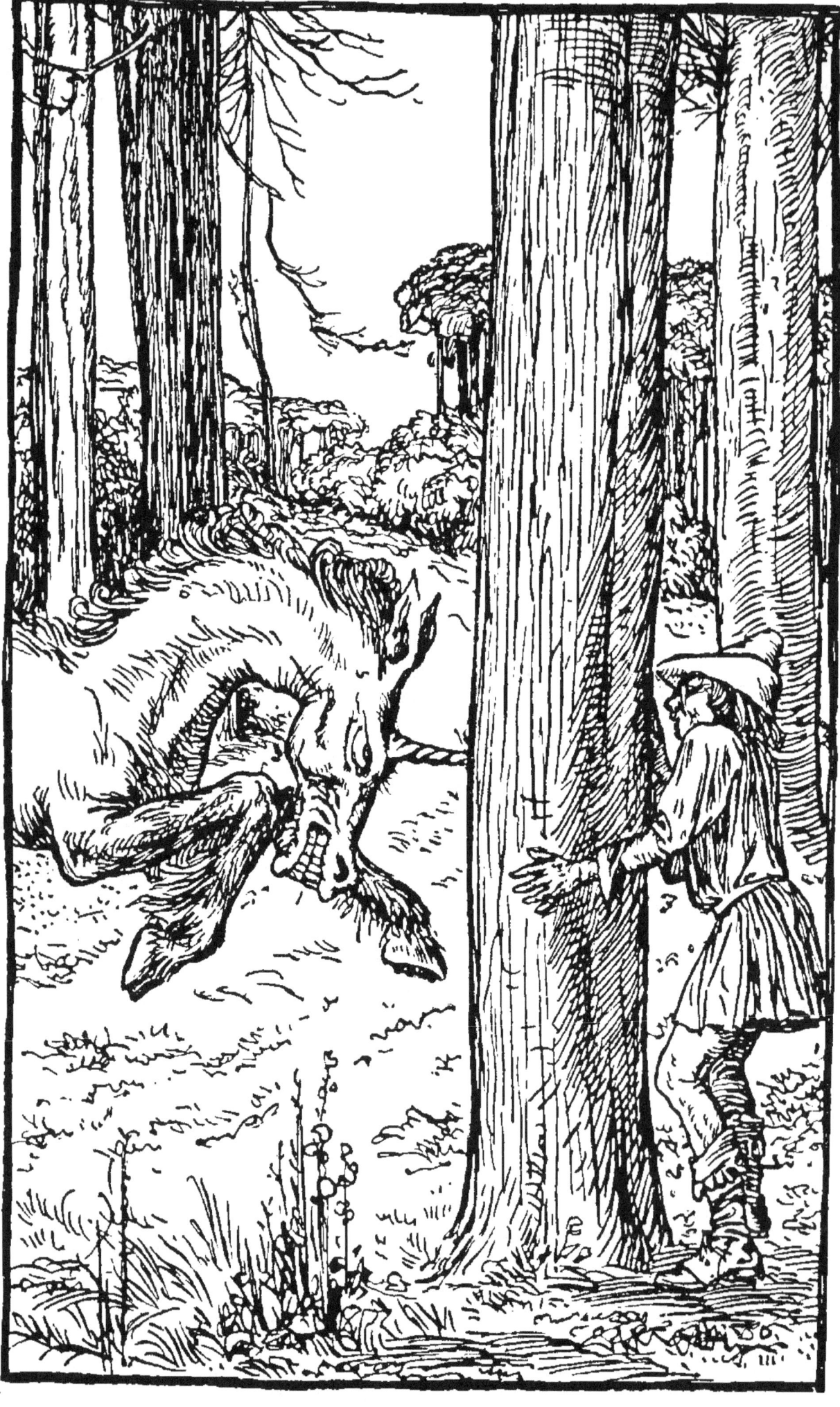

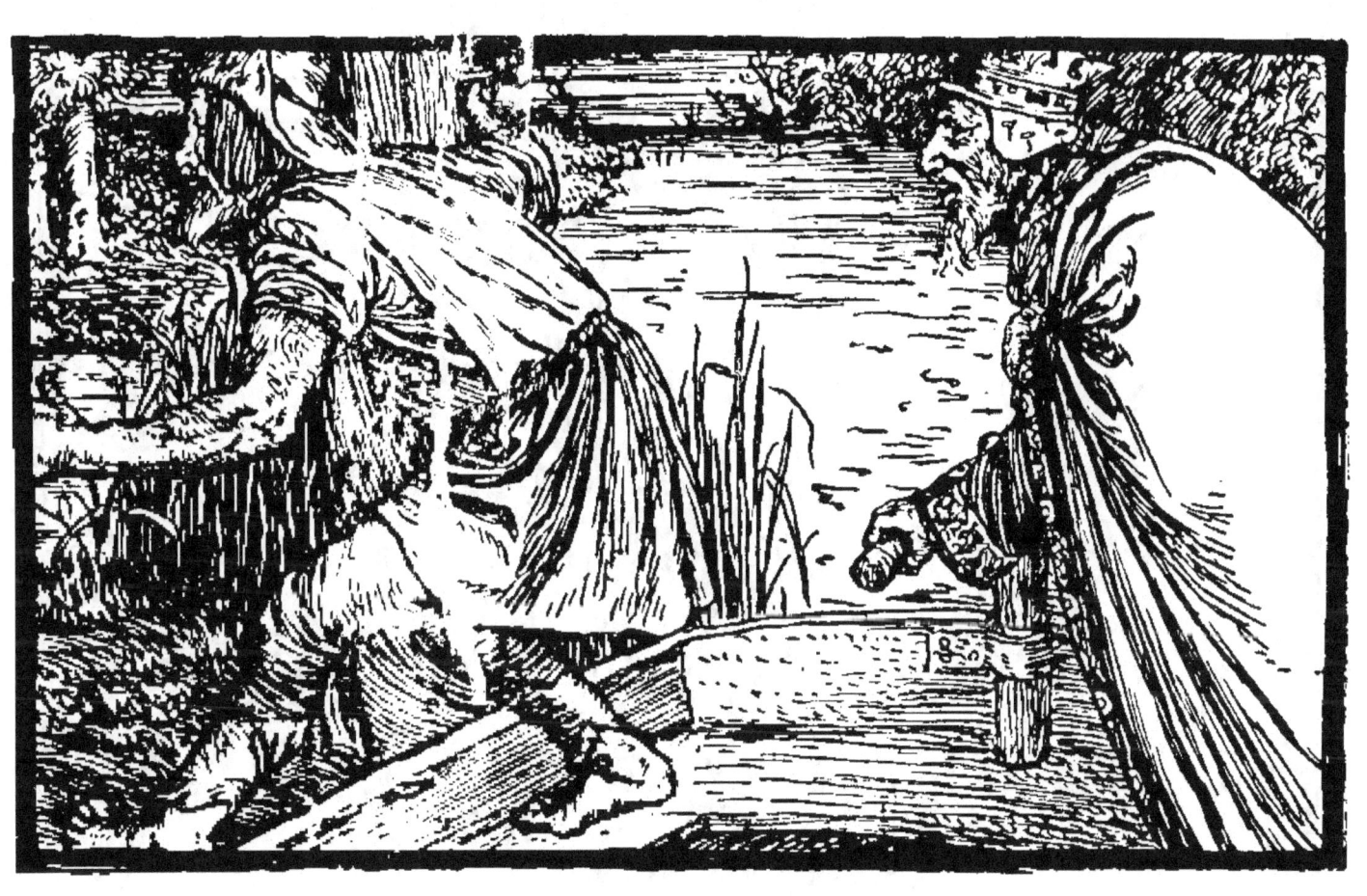

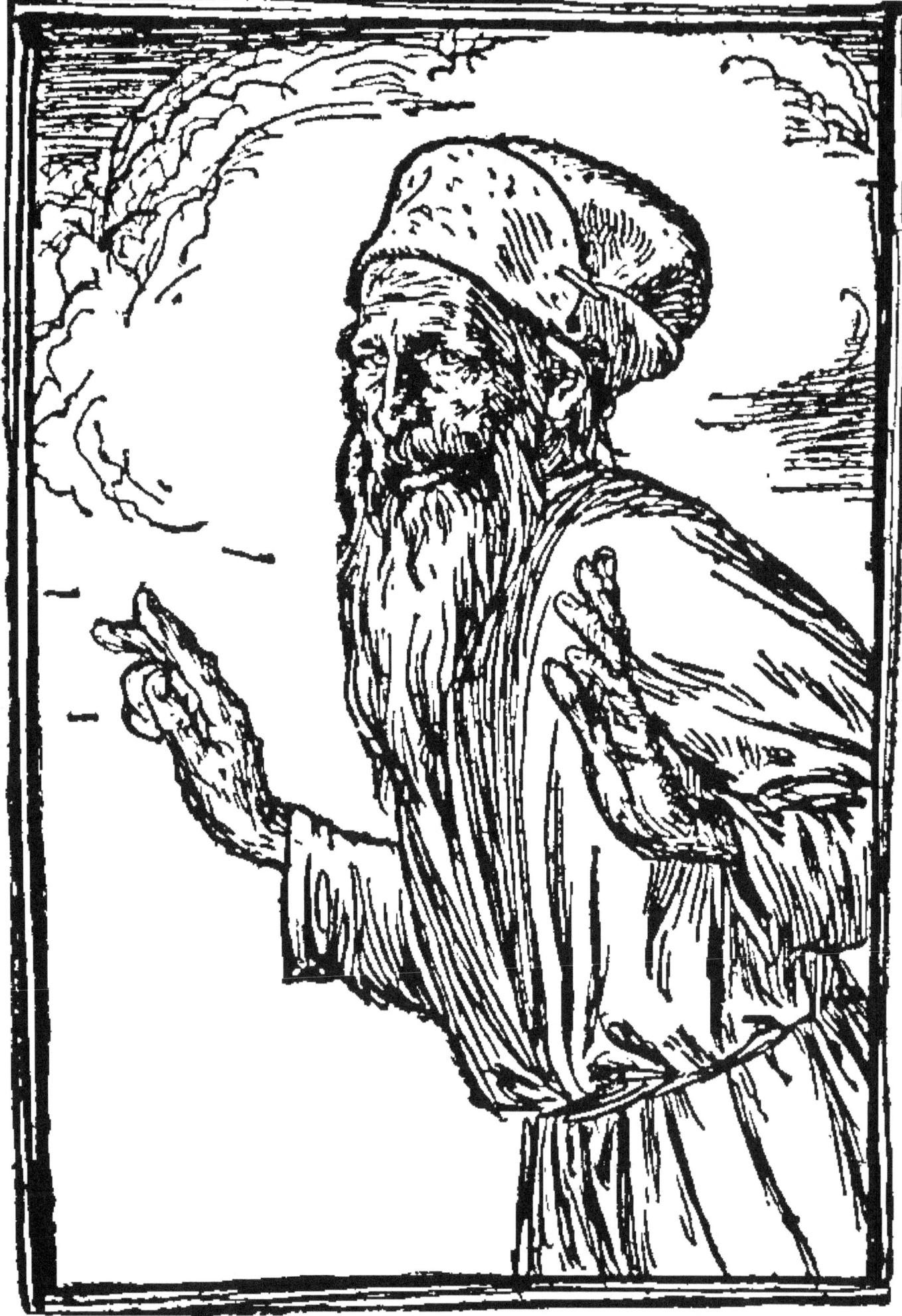

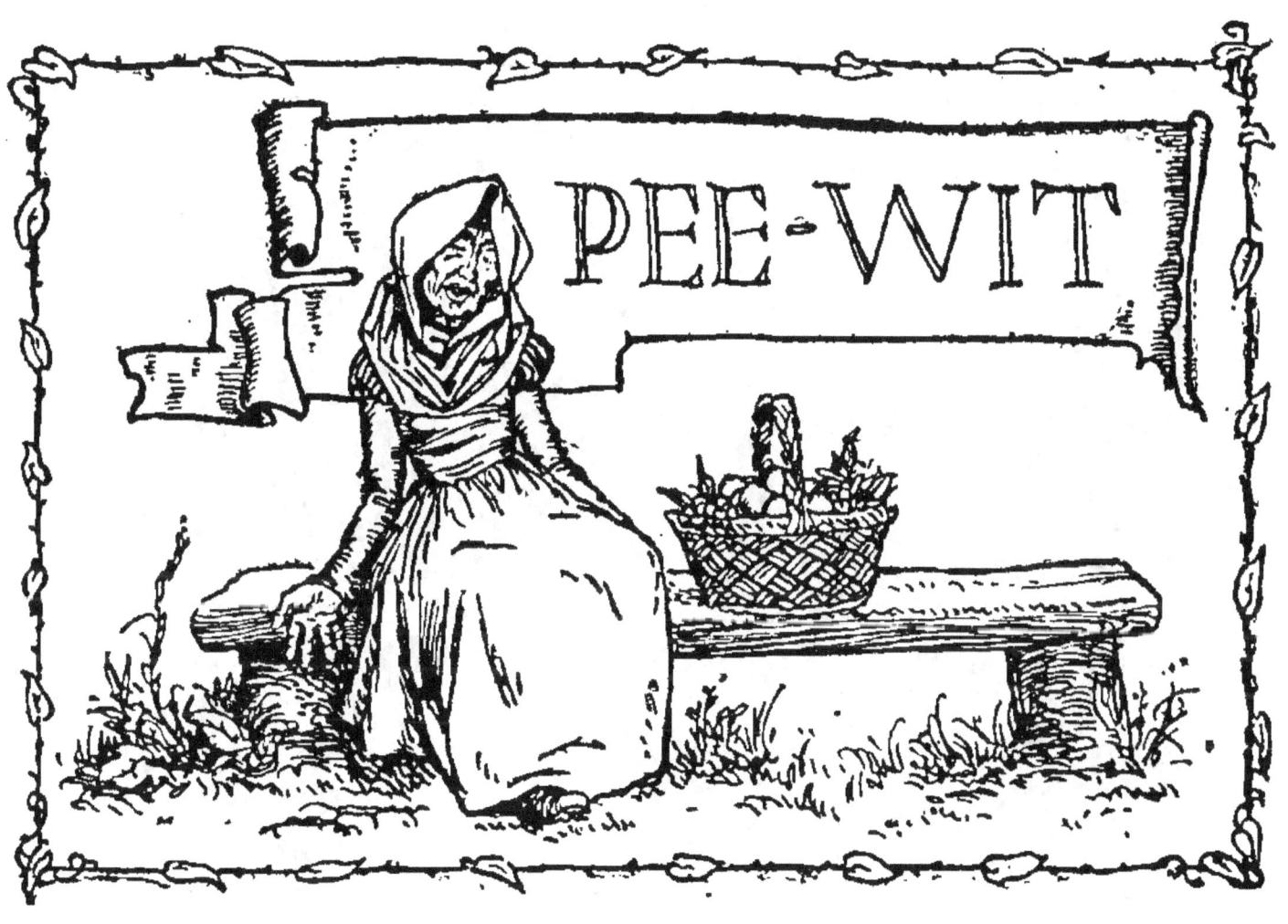

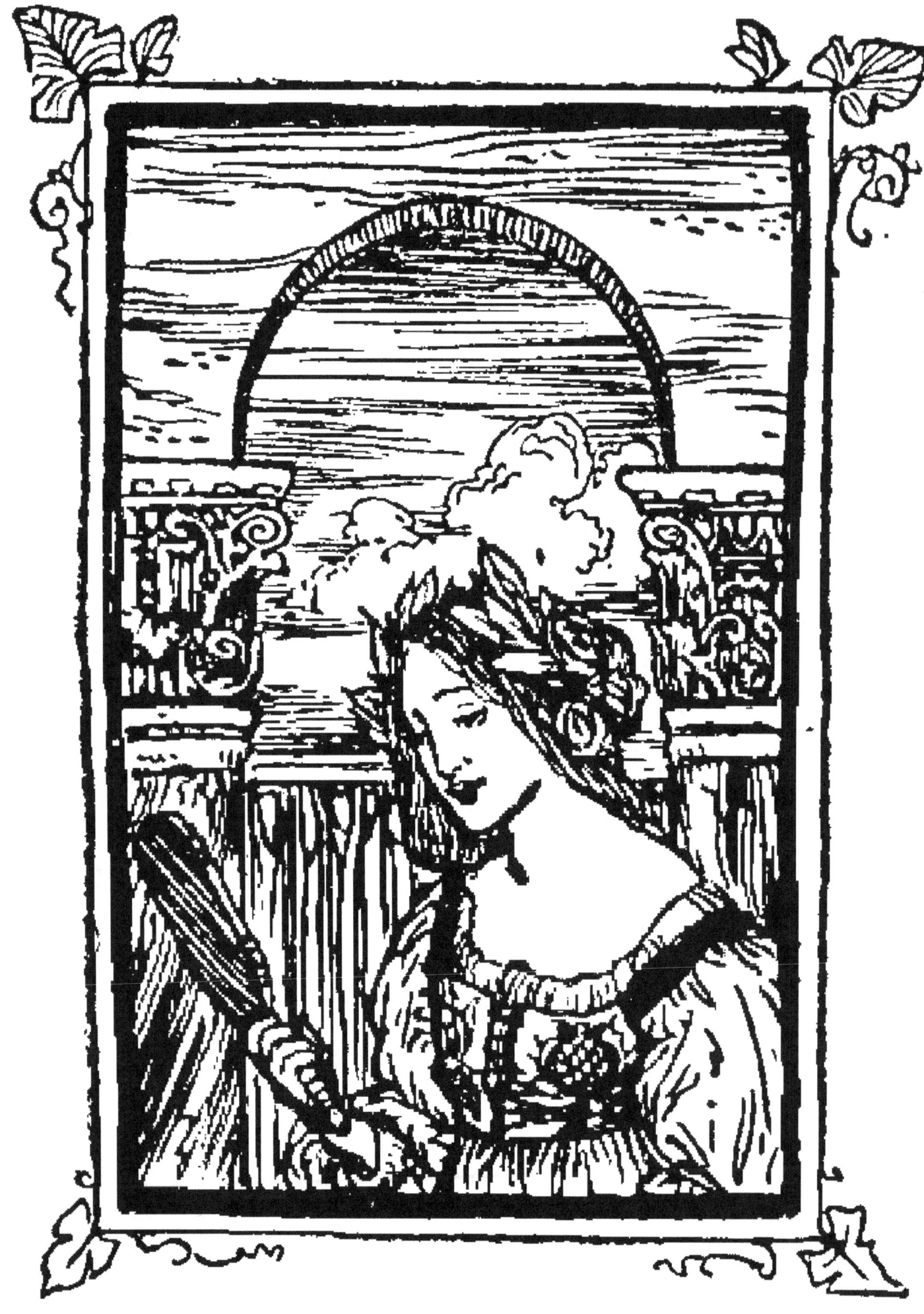

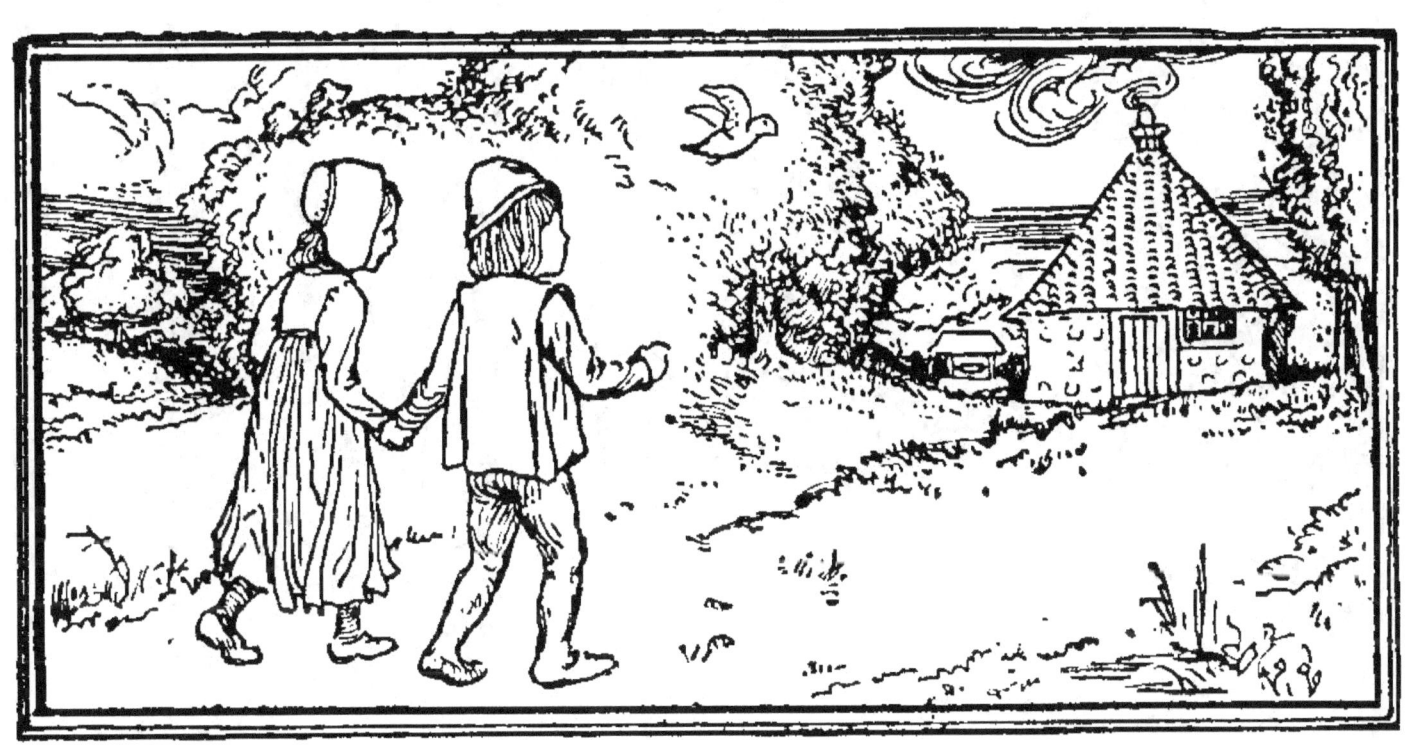

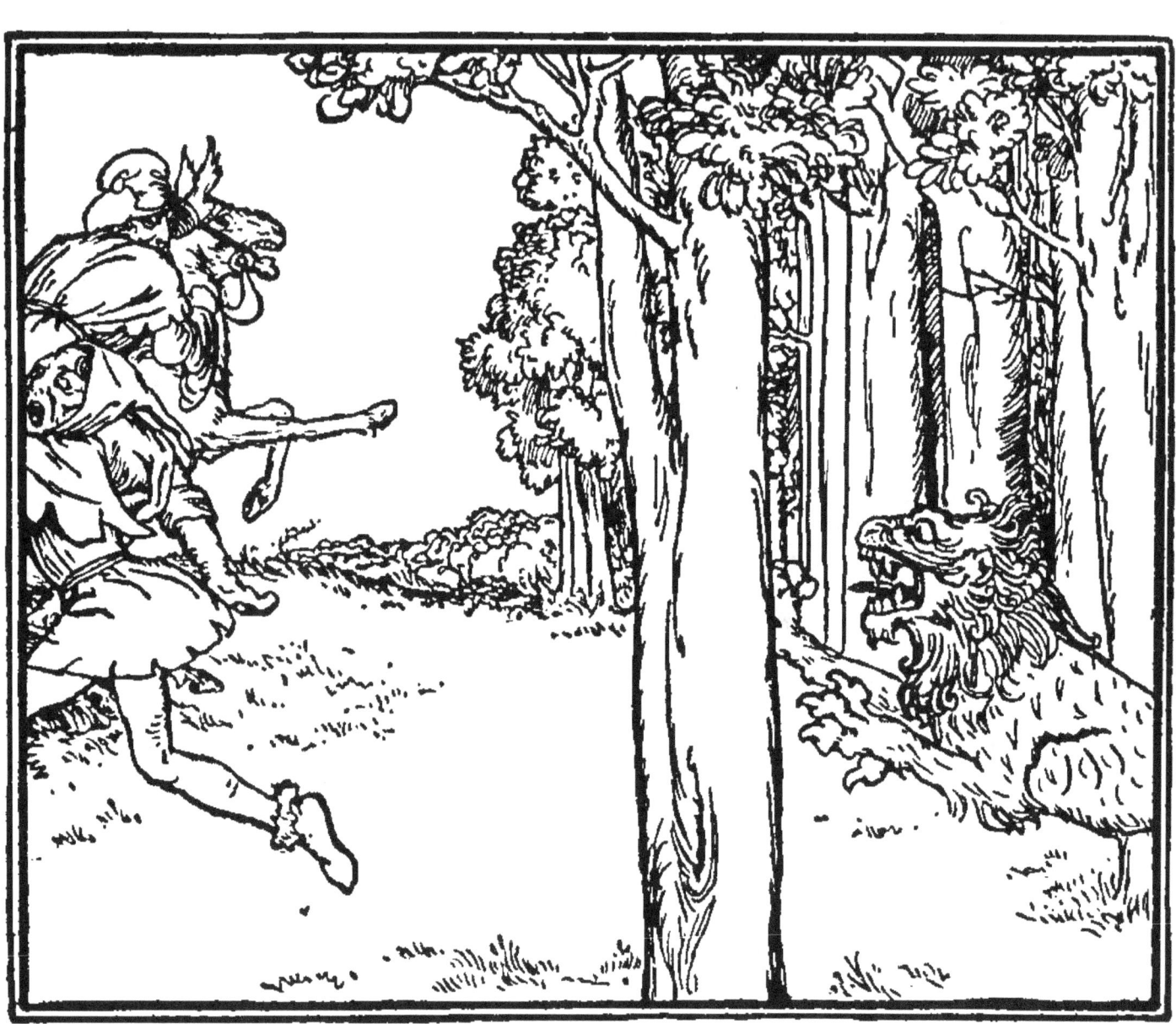

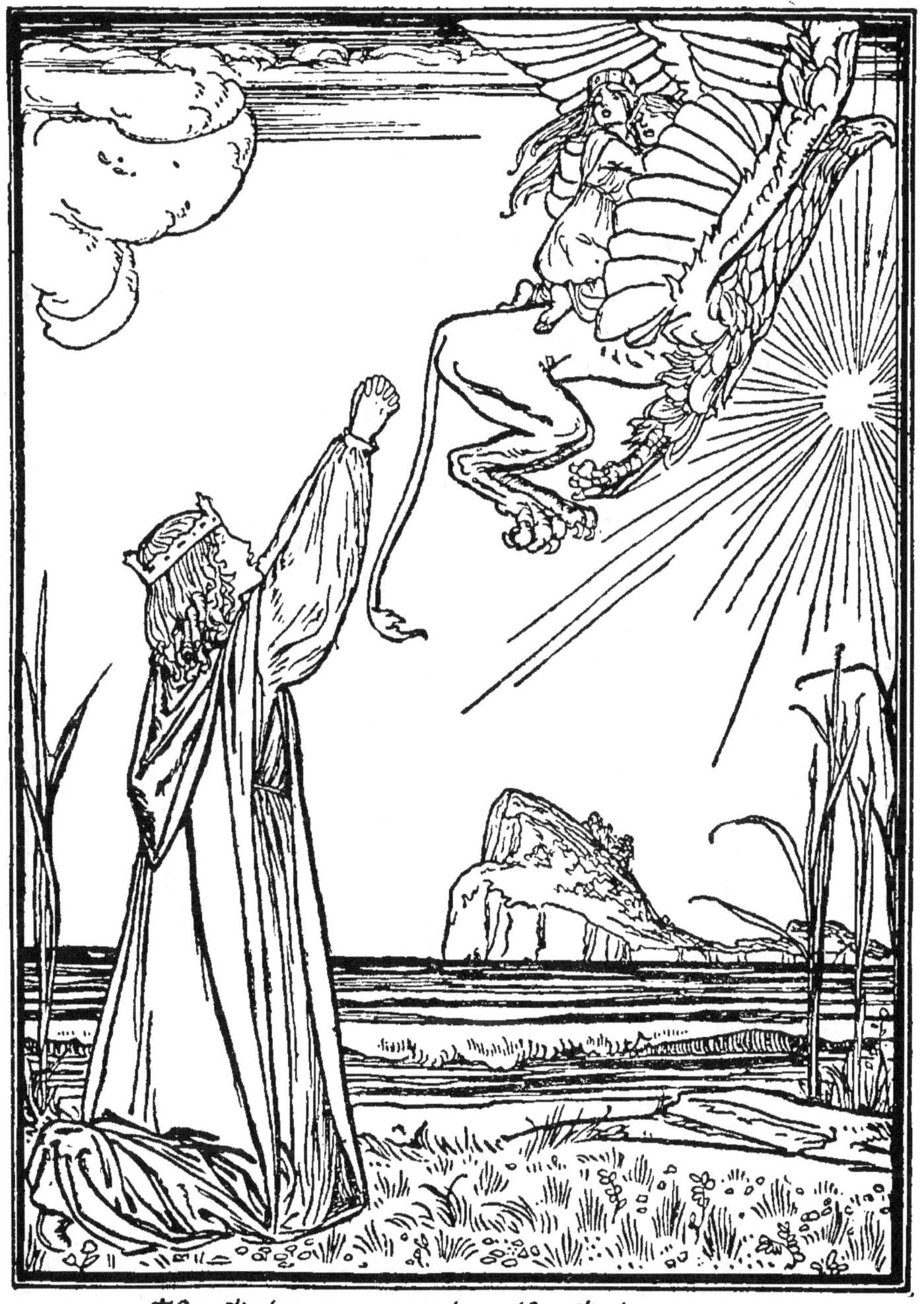

The Princess carrying the Prince away

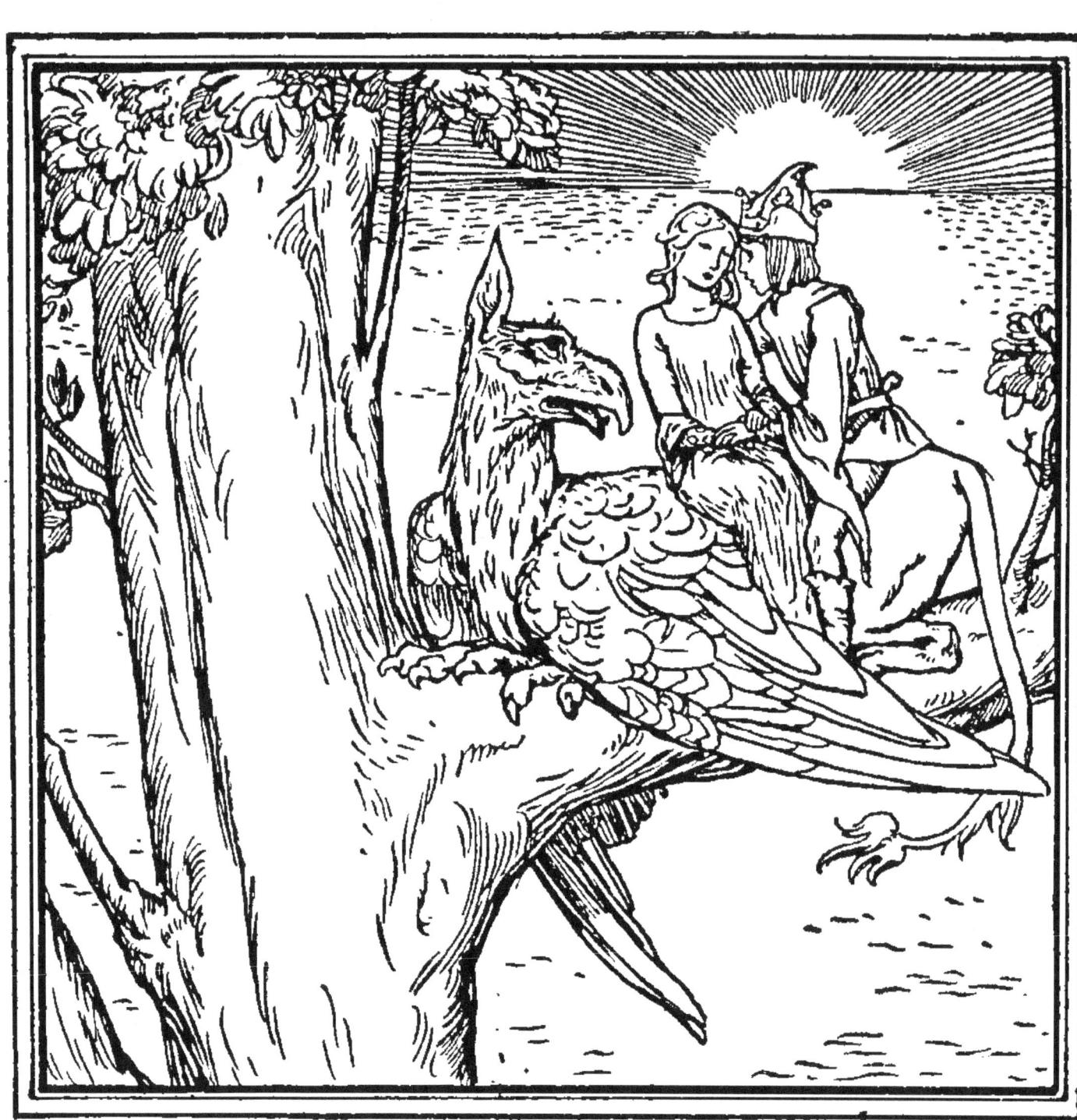

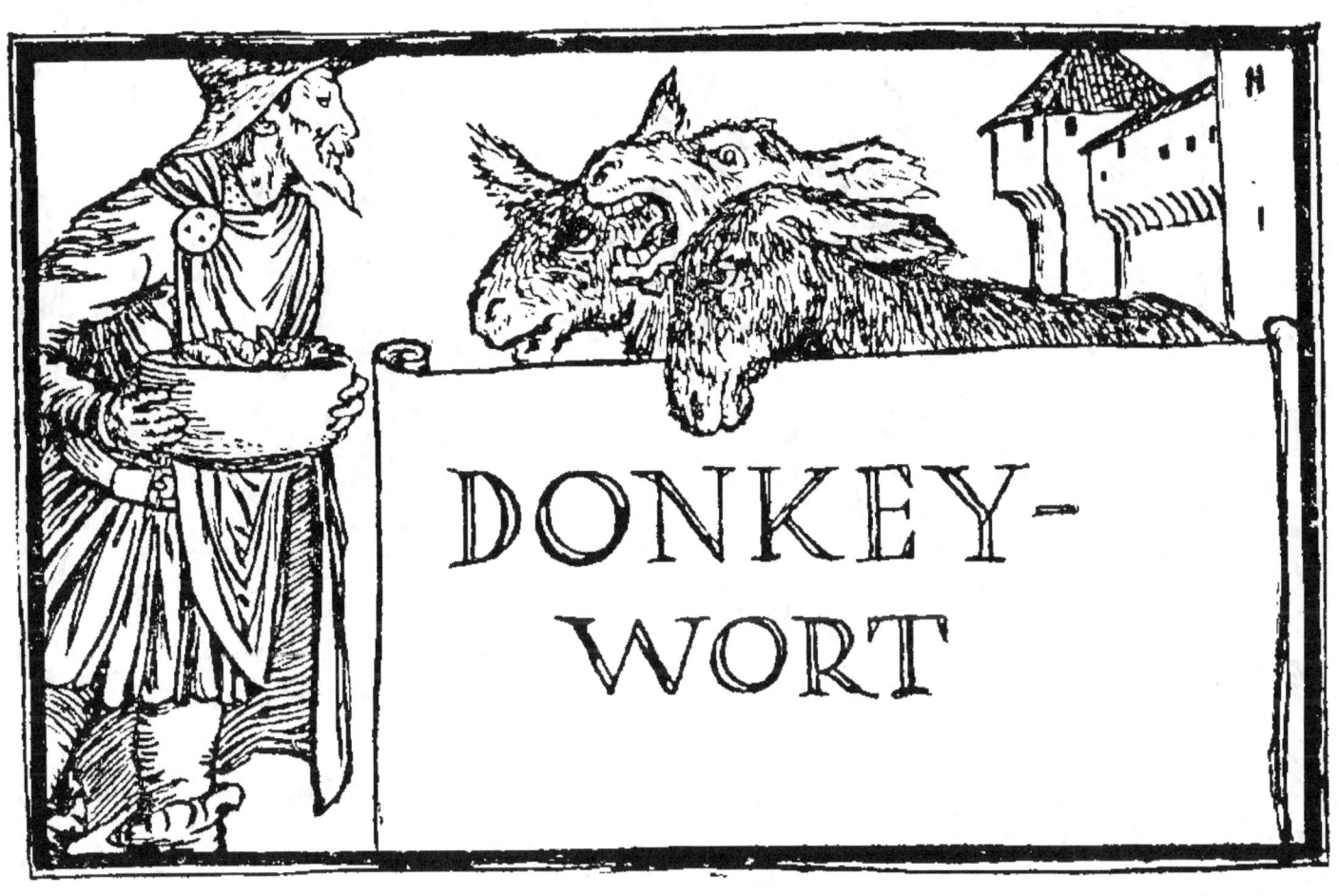

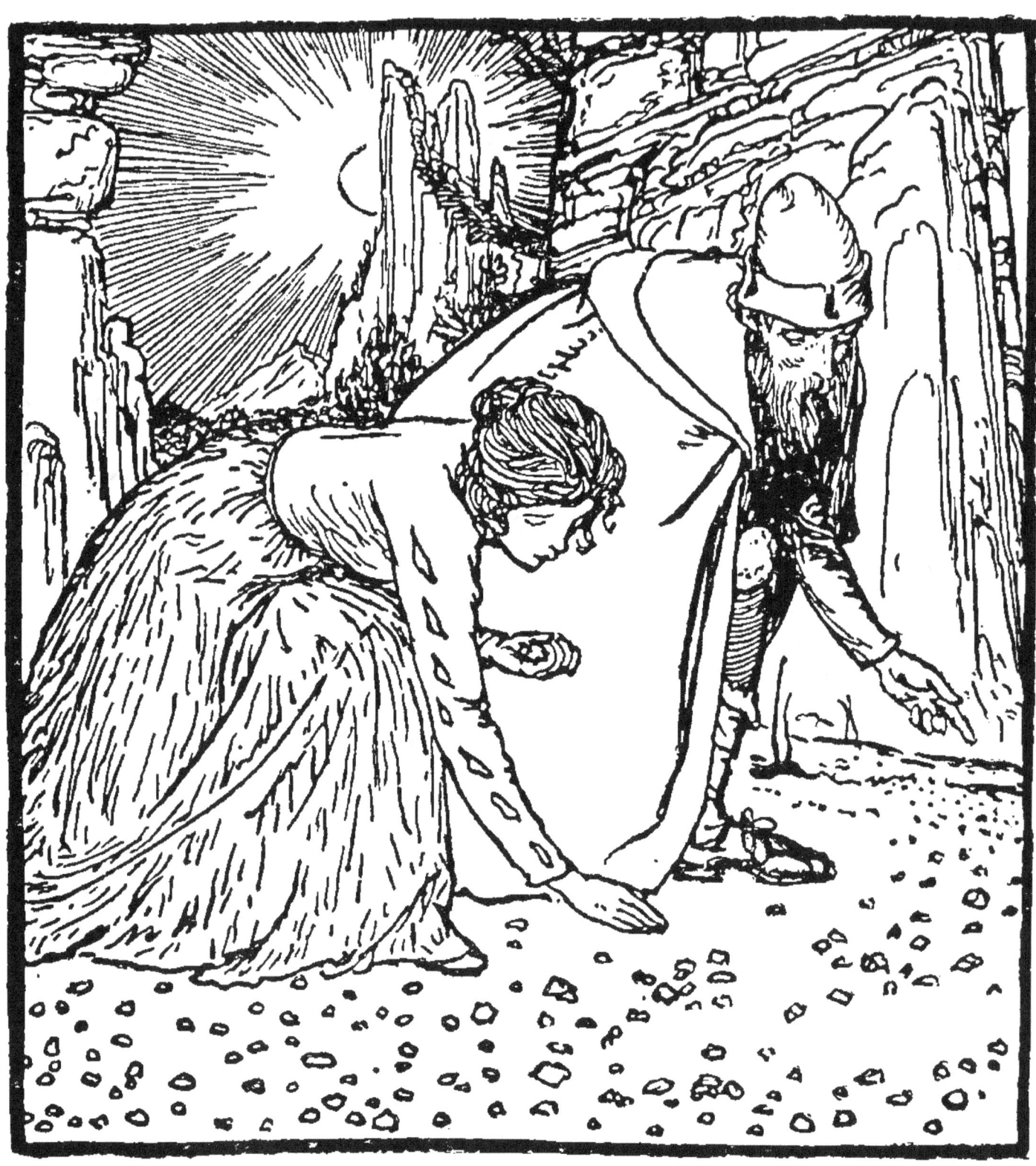

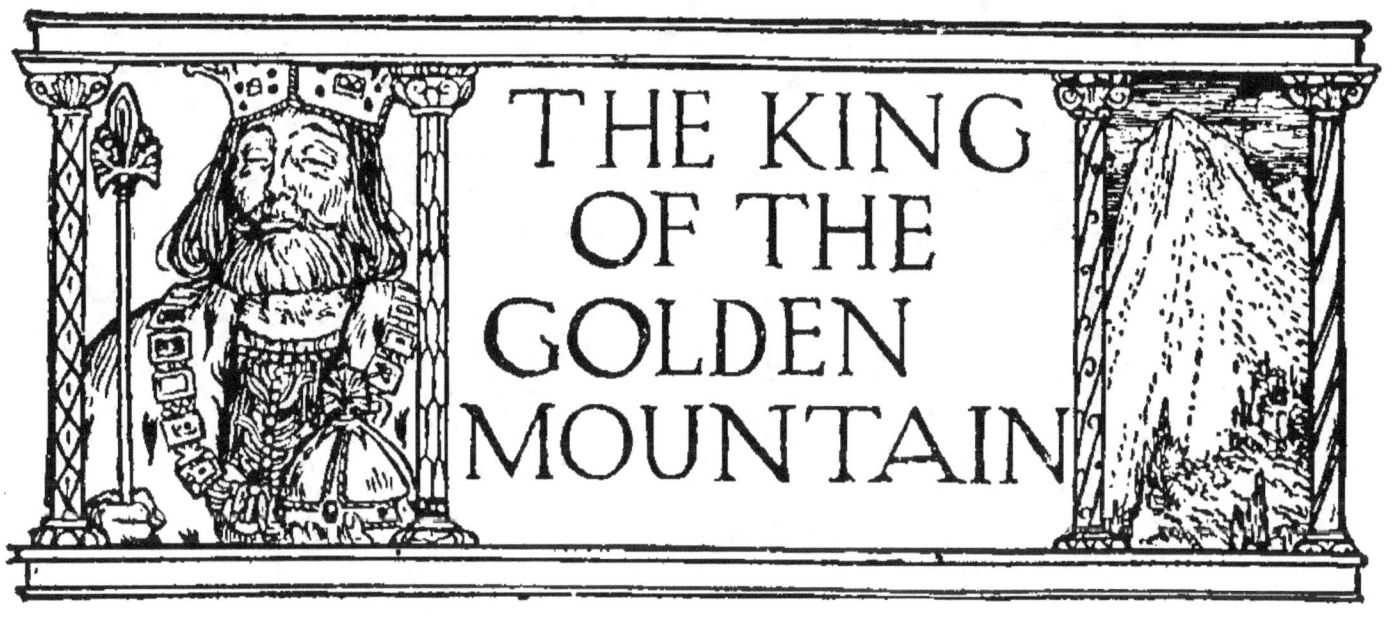

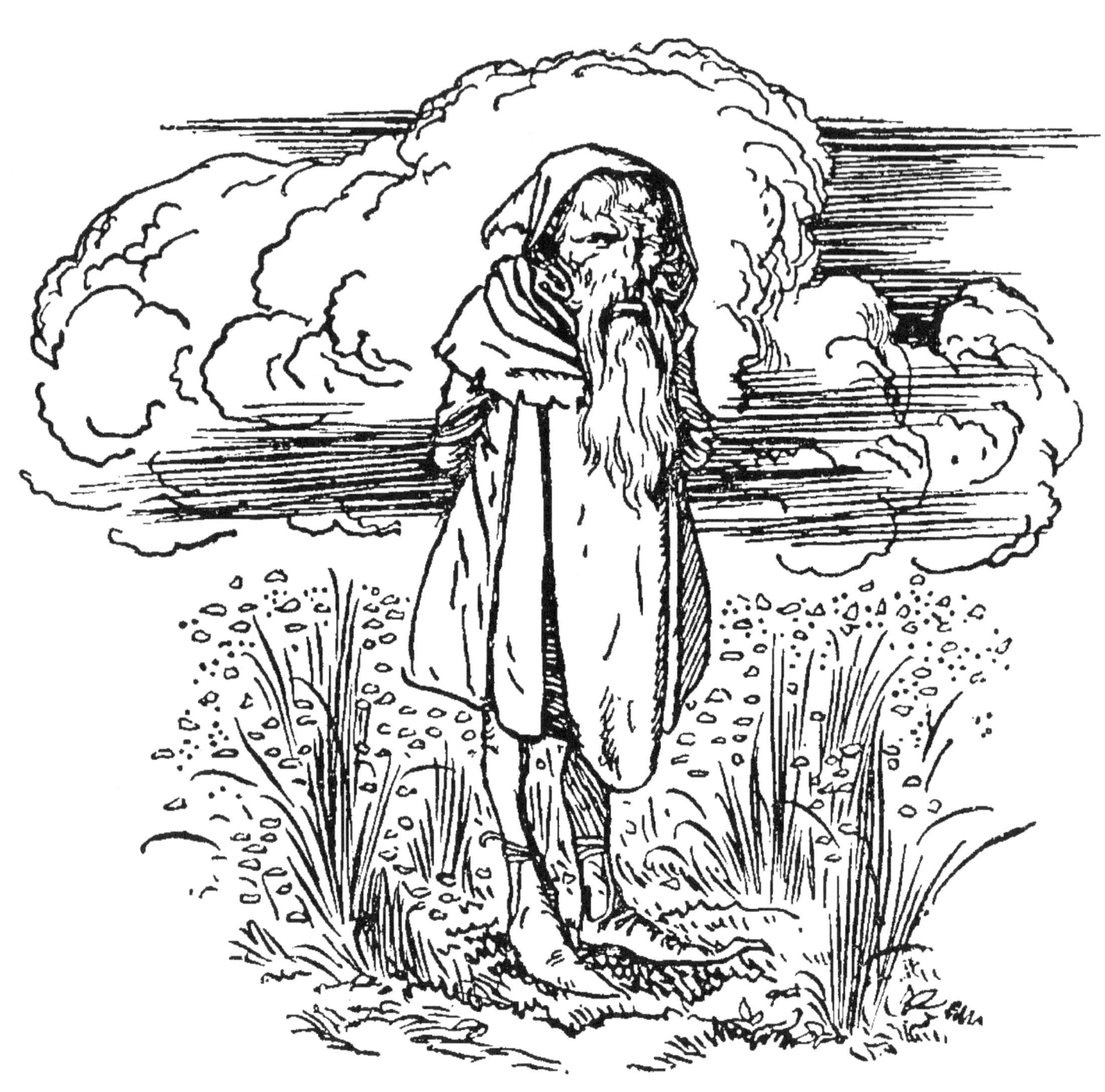

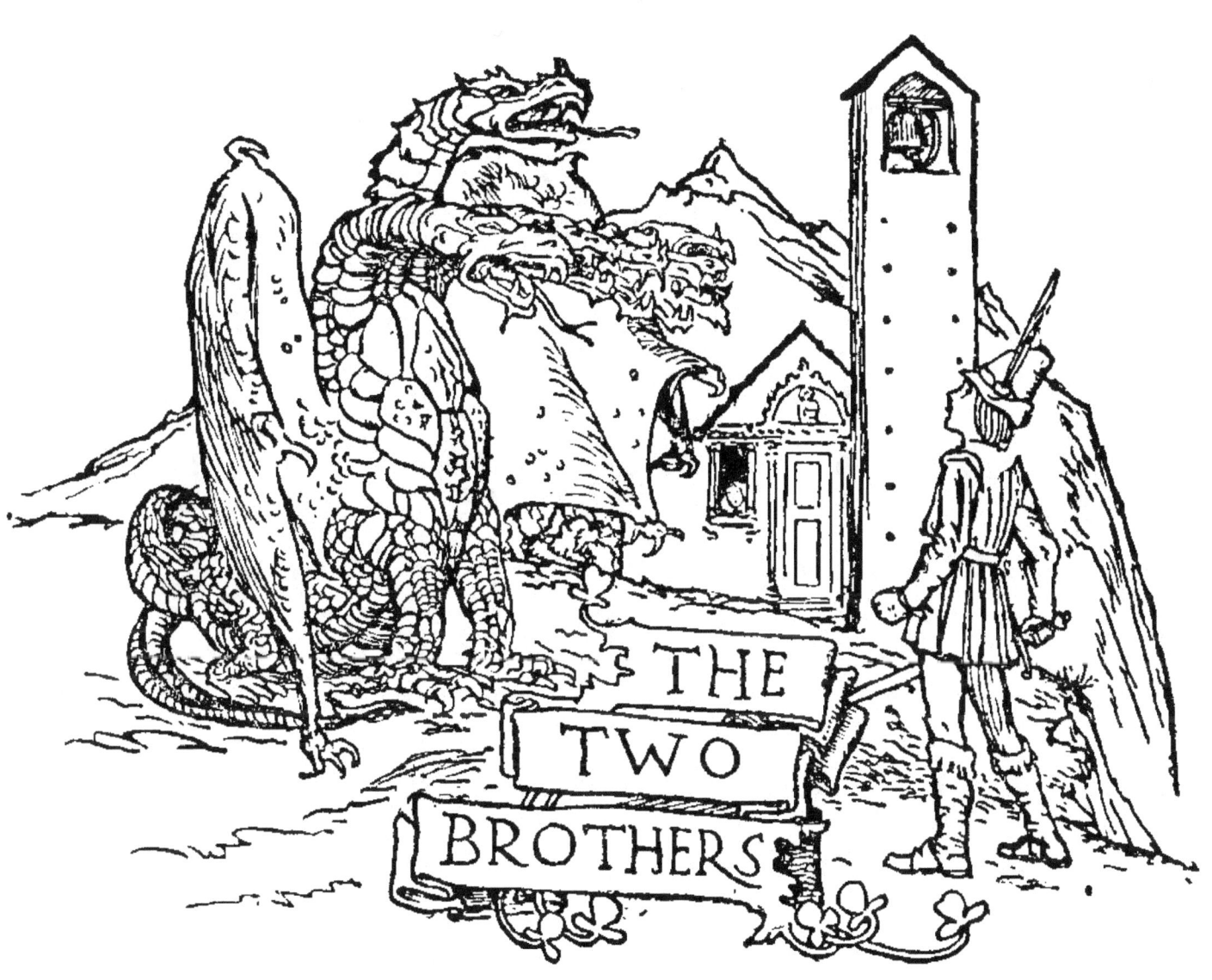

www.ingramcontent.com/pod-product-compliance
Lightning Source LLC
Chambersburg PA
CBHW082212220526
45470CB00010B/3144